Origami for Christmas

Origami
for
Christmas

Chiyo Araki

Introduction by Lillian Oppenheimer
Arrangements by Kunio Ekiguchi

KODANSHA INTERNATIONAL LTD.
Tokyo, New York, and San Francisco

The publisher would like to thank the following for their assistance: Mr. and Mrs. James Hodge, Mr. and Mrs. Larry Carter, Ms. Leila Tanaka, Ms. Ayako Nishikawa.

Photographs by Akihiko Tokue

Distributed in the United States by Kodansha International/USA Ltd., through Harper & Row, Publishers, Inc., 10 East 53rd Street, New York, New York 10022.

Published by Kodansha International Ltd., 12-21, Otowa 2-chome, Bunkyo-ku, Tokyo 112 and Kodansha International/USA Ltd., with offices at 10 East 53rd Street, New York, New York 10022 and at The Hearst Building, 5 Third Street, Suite 430, San Francisco, California 94103.

LCC 82-80736
ISBN 0-87011-528-6
ISBN 4-7700-1012-5 (in Japan)

Library of Congress Cataloging in Publication Data
Araki, Chiyo.
  Origami for Christmas.

  1. Christmas decorations. 2. Origami. I. Title.
TT900.C4A7 1983   736'.982   82-80736
ISBN 0-87011-528-6

CONTENTS

INTRODUCTION

As with many popular art forms, the origins of the Japanese art of origami—of making representational objects of paper by folding it, generally without any cutting, pasting or decorating—are obscure. According to one school of thought, it began approximately two centuries after paper-making techniques were first introduced into Japan from China via Korea in the sixth century A.D. By the eighth century, origami seems to have been firmly established, for during the annual Doll Festival, children of aristocratic families used to make dolls of paper which were thrown into the river in the belief that, just as the dolls were swept away by the current, so would any evil spirits that threatened the children.

Although paper-making soon spread throughout Japan, until recently paper was still considered a valuable commodity and origami creations were used carefully, principally for such special ceremonial purposes as the folded decorations attached to gifts—one aspect of the superb Japanese tradition of elegant and decorative gift-wrapping—and as display pieces at shrine and temple festivals. The folding techniques of these elaborate ceremonial displays were so complicated that mastery of them required extensive study with a specialist, but over the centuries they gradually evolved into the simple representational forms we see today.

The Japanese people have been brought up on origami, and recent origami exhibits are a striking testimony to the breadth, delicate beauty, and surprising realism that professional artists can achieve with the simplest of materials. For the amateur, too, origami offers a world of pleasure: even a beginner can make a few sharp folds and capture the quintessence of a flower, a bird, an animal. And therein lies the charm of this particular handicraft—with a little patience, a few sheets of paper, and the desire to create something of beauty, anyone of any age in any place in the world can enjoy the art of origami.

In this book, this most oriental of arts is applied to the most Western of holidays, Christmas. Perhaps surprisingly, the combination is completely successful. Christmas is a time for honoring traditions, for sharing, for families to gather together and enjoy themselves, nowadays often their only chance to do so in the whole year. Decorating the house and the tree is an integral part of this and origami lends itself perfectly to this joyous Western custom of creating handmade decorations for the home. Alternatively, the whole family might set out to work together to create some of the set pieces shown in this book and give them to friends as truly original Christmas gifts, gifts that will be enormously appreciated in this day and age when commercialism threatens the very spirit of Christmas.

Although origami is ancient as an art, its forms are strikingly contemporary in appearance. In fact, in addition to their grace as decorations, it is the clean and economic lines of these creations that seem especially appropriate to the simplicity that lies at the very heart of the holiday of Christmas.

LILLIAN OPPENHEIMER
Founder and Director
The Origami Center of America

GENERAL INFORMATION

This book is divided into two parts: in Part 1—*Individual Origami*, detailed, step-by-step instructions for each of the origami are presented; in Part 2—*Christmas Arrangements*, all elements, materials, and instructions necessary to make the set pieces shown in the color plates are given. Beginners should read this General Information section carefully to familiarize themselves with the terms and the diagrams used in the instructions for folding origami. A few basic suggestions will enable even a novice to become quite skillful within a short time:

1. Unless otherwise indicated, always start folding with the sheet of paper face down on the table. If the sheet of paper is colored on one side only, that color should be face down when you begin folding, so that it will be on the outside of the finished origami. Similarly, with paper with a different color on each side, the color you wish to appear on the outside should be face down when you begin.

2. Practice with scrap paper, notebook paper, or any inexpensive paper similar in weight to that suggested in the instructions.

3. Beginners should first try the simpler origami and move on to the more complicated ones when they have achieved proficiency and confidence. Some simple origami are the chicken (p. 30), the peacock (p. 32), the swan (p. 34), the dove (p. 36), the tree (p. 37), and the tulip (p. 40). After these, the crane A folds (p. 22) should be mastered since the initial steps of this design are used in many of the more creative origami. When you are comfortable with this crucial fold, other more complicated ones will be relatively easy to learn.

4. As with any other handicraft, the greatest requirement is patience. Remember that a design will become easier and take less time each time it is folded.

SIZES: The dimensions given beside the title of each of the individual origami indicate the finished size of the piece based on the size of the sheet of paper listed under "Materials." The size of the sheet is usually 6″ × 6″, which is the basic size of origami paper in Japan and is the most convenient size for practicing the folds. However, the sizes of the Christmas arrangements in Part 2 vary considerably, and you may also wish to experiment with entirely new sizes (and colors). When several origami have to fit together, as with Santa's boots and hat, it is of course necessary to coordinate the paper sizes accordingly.

With the exception of the kimono, each of the origami in this book requires a square sheet of paper. Here is an easy way to make a perfect square from a rectangular sheet of paper.

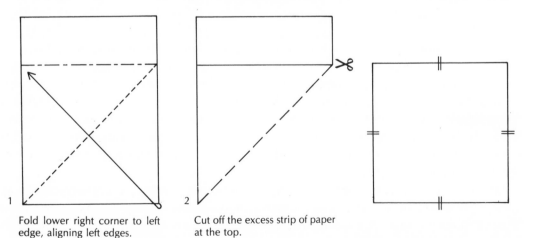

1   Fold lower right corner to left edge, aligning left edges.

2   Cut off the excess strip of paper at the top.

All dimensions are given in inches. For those who are more comfortable working in centimeters, the handy ruler on the margin of this page provides an easy system for conversion. Alternatively, you can convert inches to centimeters approximately by multiplying the number of inches by 2.5. (To convert centimeters to inches, multiply the number of centimeters by 0.4.)

THE DIAGRAMS: Below are the symbols used in the instruction diagrams.

A line of small dots indicates the fold line for that step.

A line of dashes indicates the line folded in the previous step.

— — — — — — —

A solid line indicates a previously made crease.

_____

A line of dots and dashes (i.e., a broken dotted line) is occasionally used to show the line to which the edge of the paper should be moved.

— · — — · — · — — · —

Scissors indicate a line which should be cut, up to the spot shown by the dot.

✀———————————•

Arrows show the direction of the fold.

————————————➤

Shading is occasionally used to make the diagrams clearer.

PAPER: In Japan, all stationery shops and department stores carry origami paper in a wide selection of colors and sizes, which is coated and colored on one side, and which produces especially sharp creases. In the United States origami paper can be found in Japanese specialty shops and well-stocked hobby shops in larger cities, and it may also be ordered by mail from: The Origami Center of America, 31 Union Square West, New York, NY 10003; (212) 255-0469. However, other paper can serve as a perfectly satisfactory substitute for origami paper and some suggestions for such substitutions are indicated below. In addition to the standard light weight paper needed for the individual origami designs, several of the Christmas decorations call for other types of paper, all of which can be found in Western stationery, office supply, and art supply shops.

1. Light weight paper. Origami paper or any standard weight paper, such as 20-pound offset paper, typing or letter paper, photocopy paper, and even decorative wrapping paper. This paper should be untextured and should produce sharp creases.

2. Medium weight paper. Approximately the weight and thickness of a postcard: 70- to 90-pound cover stock. Heavy watercolor art paper can also be used.

3. Cardboard. Includes ''mounting board,'' ''chip board,'' or any heavy card stock, such as that used for shoe boxes and other commercial packaging.

OTHER MATERIALS: Since some origami require a little cutting, you may wish to have a pair of scissors on hand. Also, a pencil is useful for scoring the creases, and the petals of the origami iris must be curled around a pencil. A few Christmas arrangements call for the special materials described below.

1. Glue. Any quick-drying crafts glue or a glue especially for paper can be found in most variety stores, hobby shops, art supply shops, and stationery stores.

2. Wire. Two types of wire are required for the decorations. References to ''floral wire'' refer to the colored wire used in professional floral arrangements, which is available from florists, hobby shops, and some art supply shops. If necessary, ordinary flexible wire from the hardware store can be wrapped with colored adhesive tape (available from hobby shops or art supply shops) to achieve the same effect.

The dove mobile and the white Christmas tree require ''galvanized steel wire.'' This thick, strong #20 wire can hold bends well and may be found in any hardware store.

3. Styrofoam. Styrofoam balls and wreaths are used for several decorations. While these are easily available from any hobby shop and many variety stores, you may wish to substitute your own fresh evergreen wreath in some instances.

4. Miscellaneous. Before starting to make the Christmas decorations, check the list of materials to make sure that you have everything on hand. Many items may be found in your own home, such as pins, flowerpots, needle and thread; others are easily obtainable in variety stores, such as colored ribbons and the red and gold adhesive stars used as decorations. Alternatively, you may improvise with whatever materials are available.

1. **Colorful origami ornaments.** The traditional Christmas colors of red, gold, and silver are showcased with an evergreen tree in a cheerful array of origami decorations, including reindeer, various geometric designs, cranes, and several tiny Christmas "packages."

9

2. Origami cranes. This tree has been decorated with the most representative and certainly one of the oldest of all origami folds, the crane. Symbolizing good fortune and long life, these appealing birds seem to have found a natural home in this small evergreen tree.

3. White origami tree. Bells, baskets, peacocks, reindeer, and other delightful origami hang from the wire frame of this "standing mobile," enhancing the graceful spiral effect of this unusual decoration.

4. "Lace" Christmas trees. The lacy meshed effect of these festive trees is achieved by a simple fold and some strategic cuts. An easy-to-make party decoration for room or table.

5. Nativity scene. This original origami crèche consists of Mary, the infant Jesus in a manger, the Three Wise Men, horses and camels, and the Christmas star. The scene can be moved from the table or mantel to beneath the tree after gifts have been opened.

6. **Dove mobile.** As a symbol of peace, this mobile of many colored doves is especially appropriate during the Christmas season. Though it appears to be delicate and somewhat intricate, the dove origami is one of the easiest to make.

7. **Santa Claus mobile.** This jovial Santa, whose "belly shakes like a bowl full of jelly," can be hung anywhere in the house during the Christmas season. This is a particularly good origami for a child to fold, with a little help from a parent or older brother or sister.

8. **Santa Claus and his reindeer.** This can be used as a cheery centerpiece on a table, on a fireplace mantel, at the base of a tree, or in a child's room. This charming Santa scene also makes a perfect Christmas gift for special friends and relatives.

9. Poinsettia wreath. As the traditional Christmas flower, these scarlet origami poinsettias set a holiday tone against the deep green of the origami Christmas holly. A lovely door or window wreath, as well as a very special Christmas gift.

10. Persimmon wreath. The motif of this sparkling door decoration is the winter-harvested oriental persimmon. The traditional persimmon fold requires no cutting; these are made of gold paper with a dark gold stripe, and are affixed to a styrofoam wreath base.

11. Wreath of white swans. This is a tasteful blend of the stylized Japanese representation of the swan and the traditional Christmas wreath. Again, a styrofoam base is used. Each swan only takes a couple of minutes to fold, and pinking shears are used to achieve the scalloped effect on the tails.

12. **Crane wreath.** These bright red and gold cranes signifying ''a life of a thousand years'' are beautifully highlighted against the deep green of an artificial evergreen wreath, achieving a lovely blend of East and West.

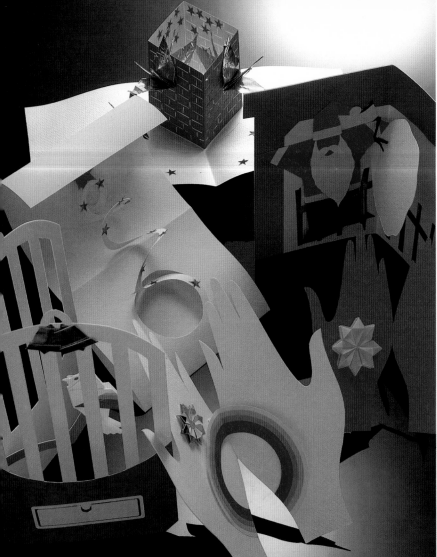

13. **Holiday greeting cards.** The whole family can participate in producing special personalized Christmas cards this year. Folds and cuts of varying levels of difficulty are represented in these cards. Included are a pop-up chimney with cranes, praying hands, a pop-out bird in a cage, a Santa with a movable bag, and a poinsettia spiral design.

14. **Origami gift wrappings.** The versatility of origami and the centuries-old Japanese heritage of beautiful gift wrappings are evident in this display of gaily decorated Christmas presents: a camellia package with a rose in the center, a persimmon decoration, poinsettias, and a chrysanthemum wrapping for small flat gifts.

15. **Flower ball ornaments.** These beautiful origami flower balls will grace any Christmas tree or table arrangement. They are made by affixing small origami flowers with wire stems to a styrofoam ball base.

16. **Festive bouquet.** This colorful array of origami flowers will continue to "bloom" well into the New Year. Included are irises, roses, and other small flowers.

17. Church scene. The purity and beauty of Christmas are subtly captured in the simple, clean lines of this set piece, a traditional scene with a fresh, contemporary flavor.

PART 1
INDIVIDUAL ORIGAMI

Detailed, step-by-step instructions for each origami.

CRANE A (3″ high, 6″ long)

MATERIALS: 1 sheet of 6″ × 6″ paper

(see also pp. 124, 136, and 139 for suggested color, weight, and size)

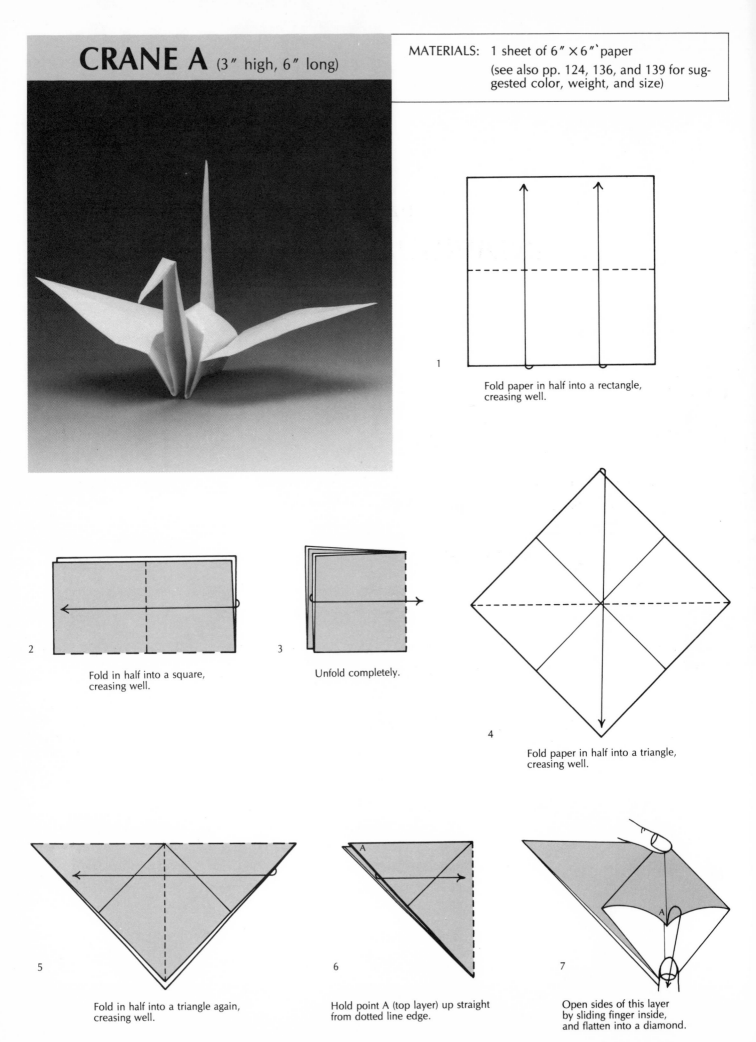

1 Fold paper in half into a rectangle, creasing well.

2 Fold in half into a square, creasing well.

3 Unfold completely.

4 Fold paper in half into a triangle, creasing well.

5 Fold in half into a triangle again, creasing well.

6 Hold point A (top layer) up straight from dotted line edge.

7 Open sides of this layer by sliding finger inside, and flatten into a diamond.

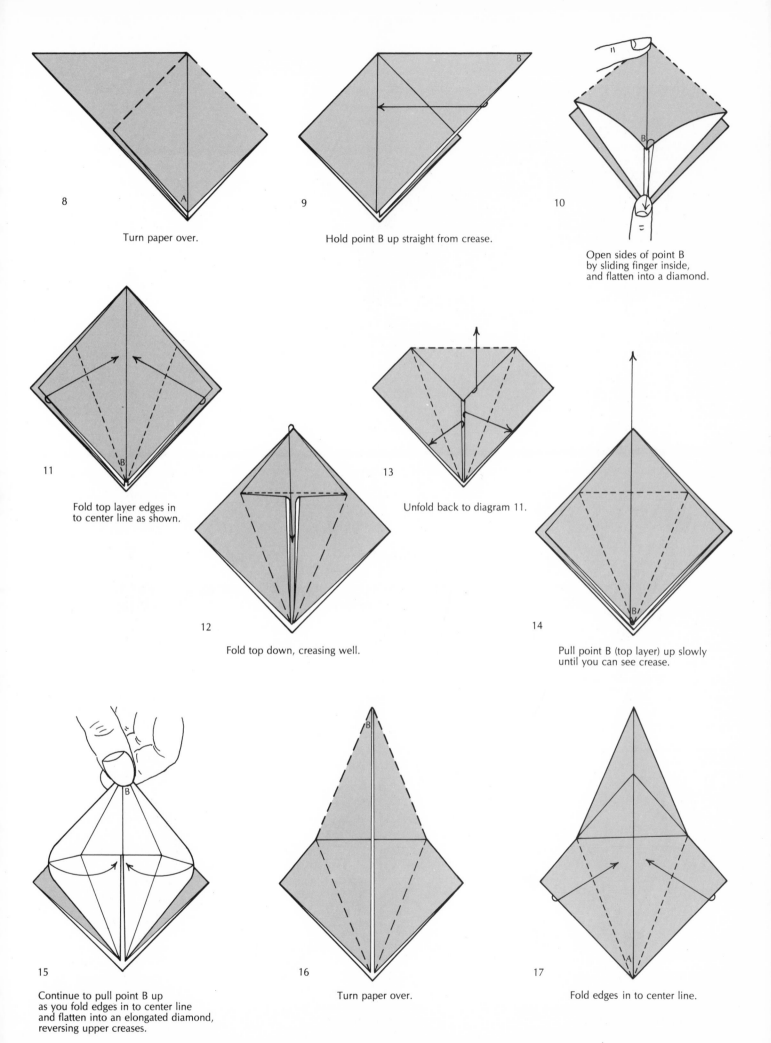

8

Turn paper over.

9

Hold point B up straight from crease.

10

Open sides of point B
by sliding finger inside,
and flatten into a diamond.

11

Fold top layer edges in
to center line as shown.

12

Fold top down, creasing well.

13

Unfold back to diagram 11.

14

Pull point B (top layer) up slowly
until you can see crease.

15

Continue to pull point B up
as you fold edges in to center line
and flatten into an elongated diamond,
reversing upper creases.

16

Turn paper over.

17

Fold edges in to center line.

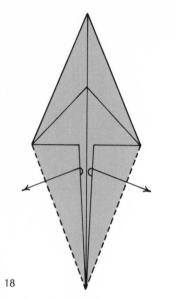

18

Unfold back to diagram 17.

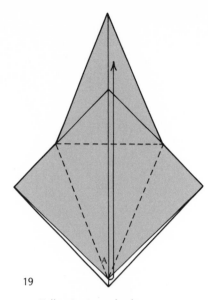

19

Pull point A up slowly
until you can see upper crease.

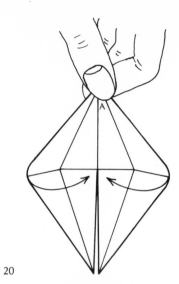

20

Continue to pull point A up
as you fold edges in to center line
and flatten into a diamond.

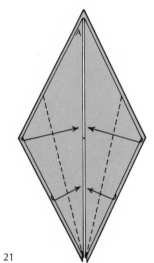

21

Fold edges in to center line.

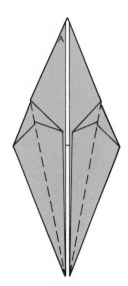

22

Turn paper over, and repeat step 21.

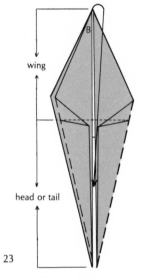

wing

head or tail

23

Fold point B (top layer) down
as far as it will go.

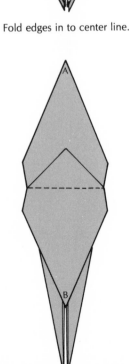

24

Turn paper over, and repeat step 23.

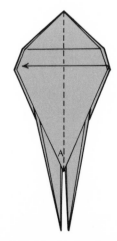

25

Fold right side (top layer)
to the left.

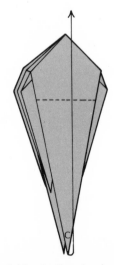

26

Fold point C up (top layer)
as far as it will go.

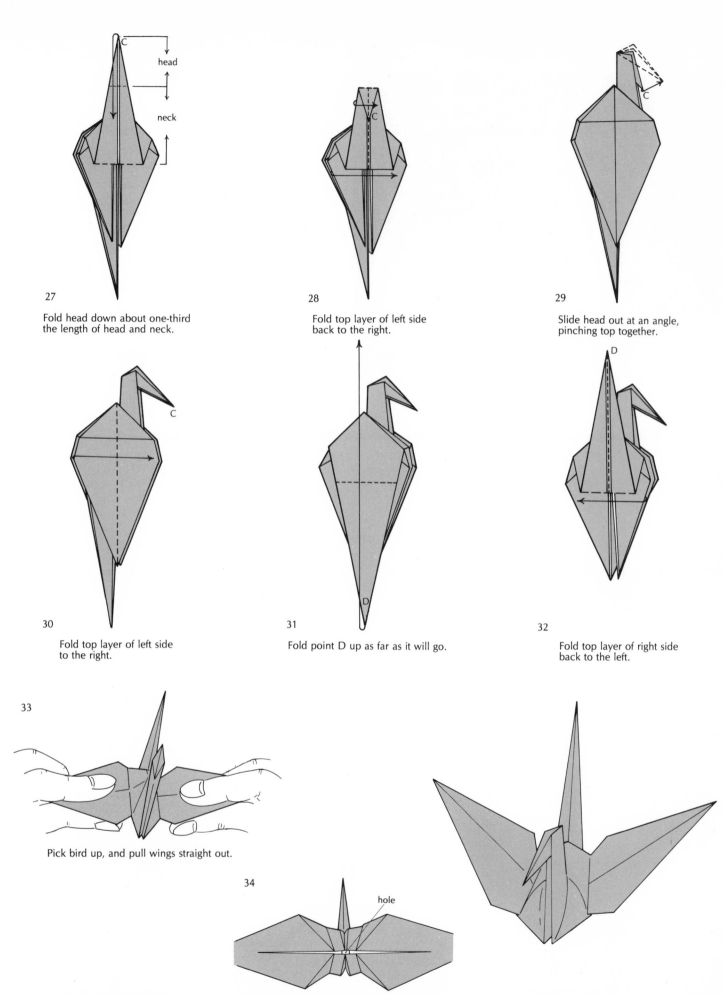

27

Fold head down about one-third the length of head and neck.

28

Fold top layer of left side back to the right.

29

Slide head out at an angle, pinching top together.

30

Fold top layer of left side to the right.

31

Fold point D up as far as it will go.

32

Fold top layer of right side back to the left.

33

Pick bird up, and pull wings straight out.

34

hole

Turn bird over, and inflate by blowing into small hole in stomach.

CRANE B (3″ high)

MATERIALS: 1 sheet of 6″ × 6″ paper

(see also p. 124 for suggested color, weight, and size)

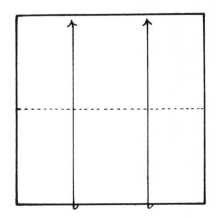

1 Fold paper in half into a rectangle, creasing well.

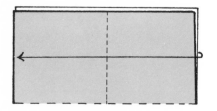

2 Fold in half into a square, creasing well.

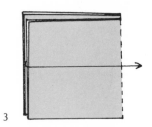

3 Unfold completely.

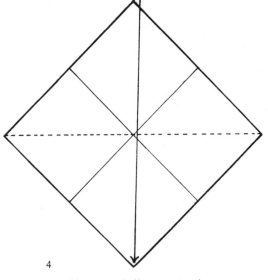

4 Fold paper in half into a triangle, creasing well.

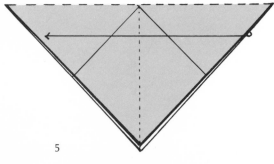

5 Fold in half into a triangle again, creasing well.

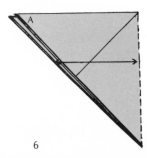

6 Hold point A (top layer) up straight from dotted line edge.

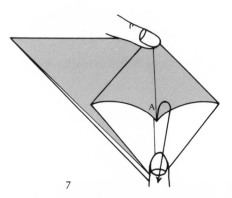

7 Open sides of this layer by sliding finger inside, and flatten into a diamond.

26

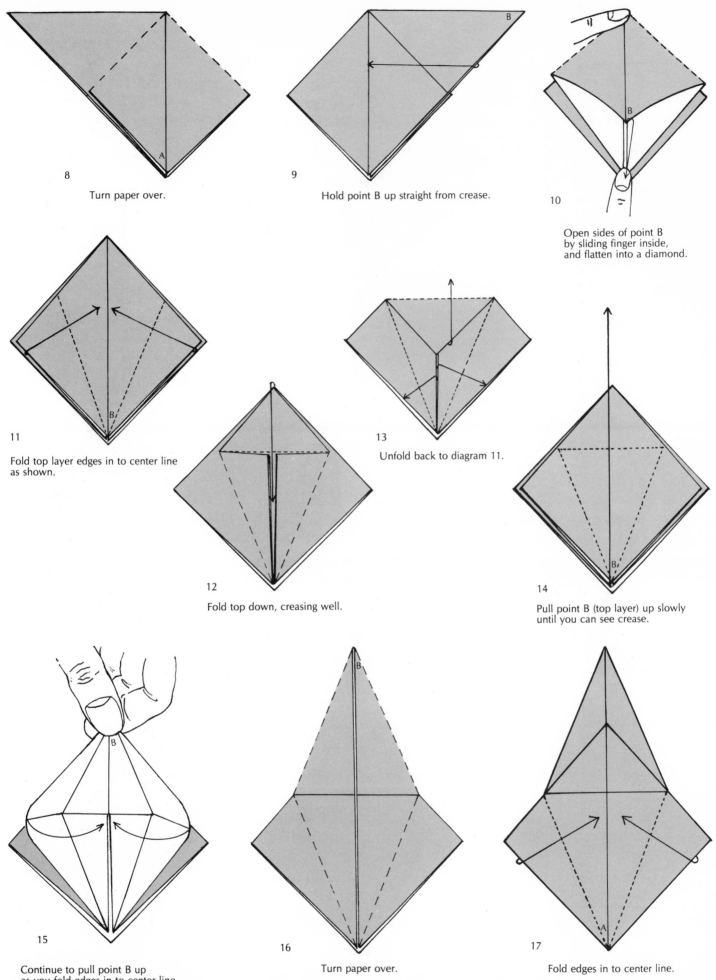

8

Turn paper over.

9

Hold point B up straight from crease.

10

Open sides of point B
by sliding finger inside,
and flatten into a diamond.

11

Fold top layer edges in to center line
as shown.

12

Fold top down, creasing well.

13

Unfold back to diagram 11.

14

Pull point B (top layer) up slowly
until you can see crease.

15

Continue to pull point B up
as you fold edges in to center line
and flatten into an elongated diamond,
reversing upper creases.

16

Turn paper over.

17

Fold edges in to center line.

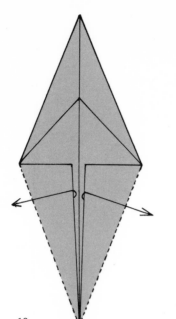

18

Unfold back to diagram 17.

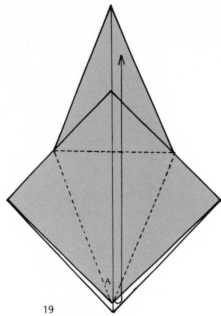

19

Pull point A up slowly
until you can see upper crease.

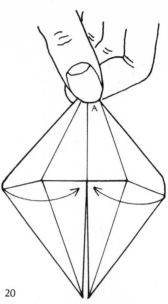

20

Continue to pull point A up
as you fold edges in to center line
and flatten into a diamond.

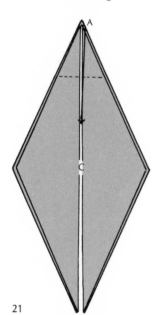

21

Fold point A (top layer) down
one-third the length of AC.

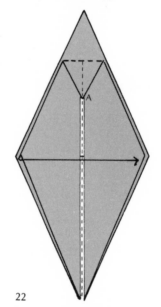

22

Fold left side (top layer) to the right.

23

Turn paper over.

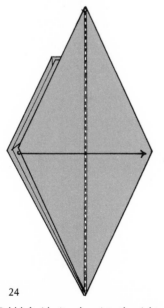

24

Fold left side (top layer) to the right.

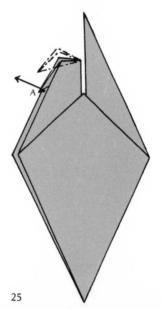

25

Slide head (A) out at an angle,
pressing top together.

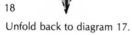

26

Divide wing into five equal parts,
and fold bottom edge up to line 1.

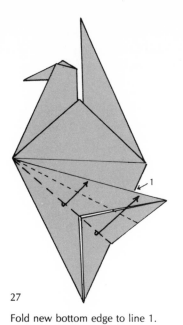

27

Fold new bottom edge to line 1.

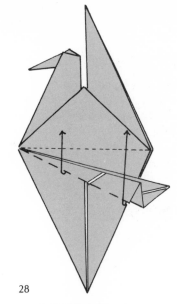

28

Fold folded wing up.

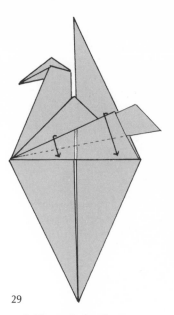

29

Fold top of wing down.

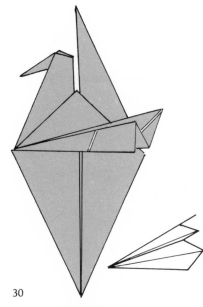

30

Unfold wing completely.

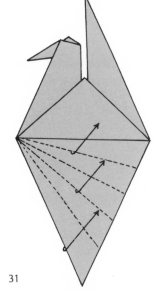
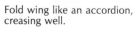

31

Fold wing like an accordion, creasing well.

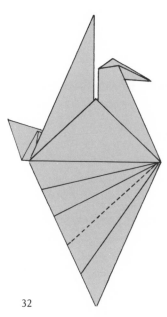

32

Turn paper over, and repeat steps 26–31.

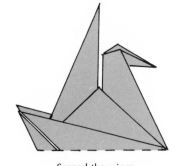

33

Spread the wings.

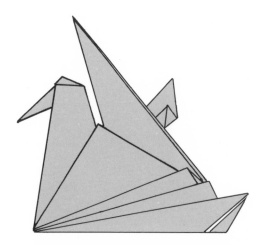

CHICKEN (3″ high)

MATERIALS: 1 sheet of 6″ × 6″ paper
(see also p. 124 and p. 126 for suggested color, weight, and size)

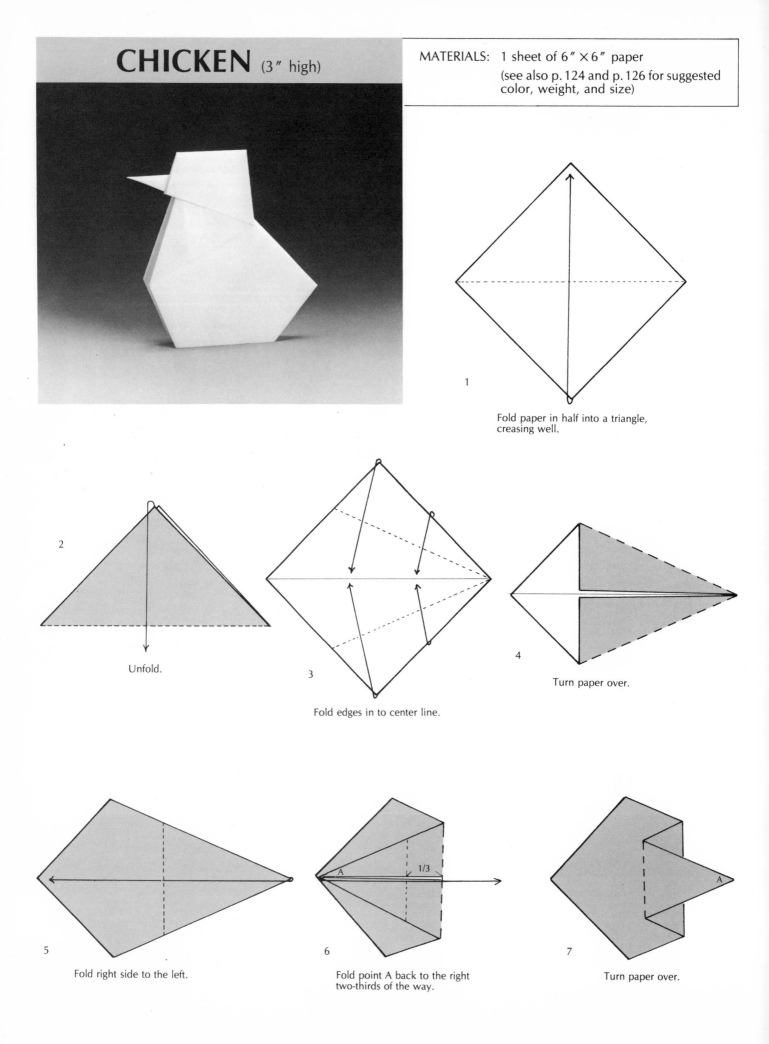

1

Fold paper in half into a triangle, creasing well.

2

Unfold.

3

Fold edges in to center line.

4

Turn paper over.

5

Fold right side to the left.

6

Fold point A back to the right two-thirds of the way.

1/3

A

7

Turn paper over.

A

30

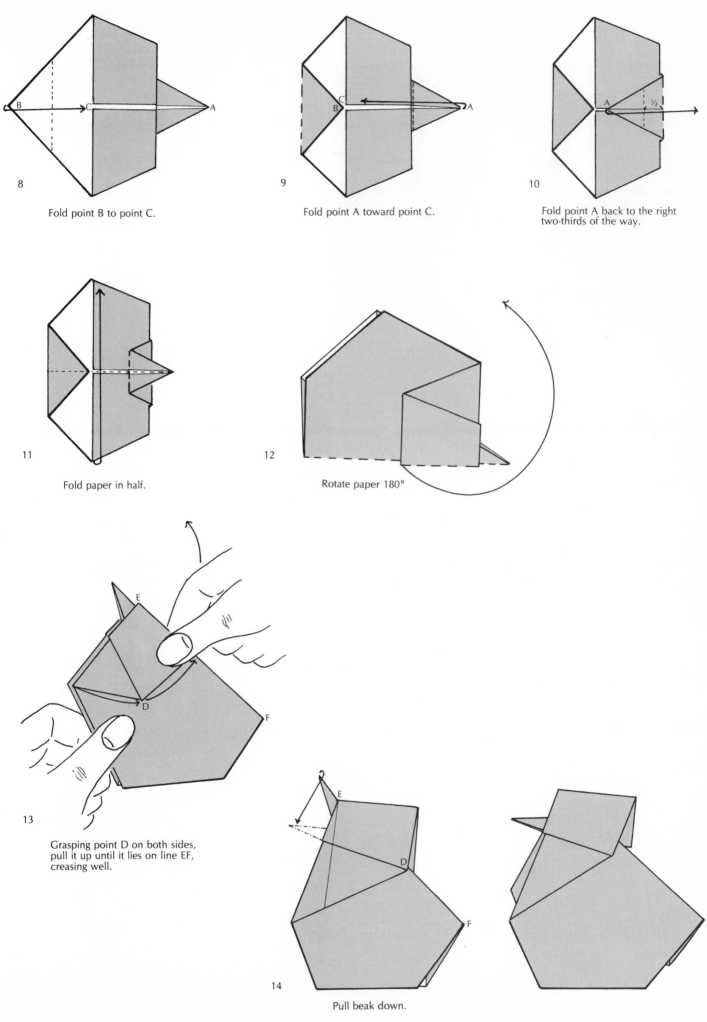

8　Fold point B to point C.

9　Fold point A toward point C.

10　Fold point A back to the right two-thirds of the way.

11　Fold paper in half.

12　Rotate paper 180°

13　Grasping point D on both sides, pull it up until it lies on line EF, creasing well.

14　Pull beak down.

PEACOCK (4½″ high)

MATERIALS: 1 sheet of 6″ × 6″ paper
(see also p. 124 and p. 126 for suggested color, weight, and size)

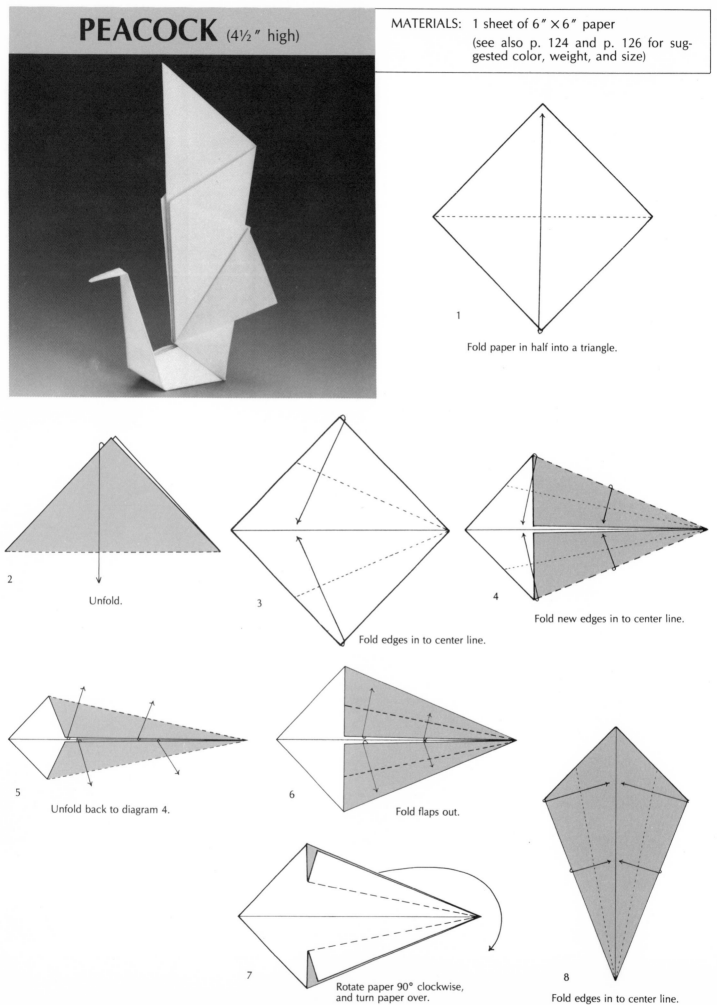

1 Fold paper in half into a triangle.

2 Unfold.

3 Fold edges in to center line.

4 Fold new edges in to center line.

5 Unfold back to diagram 4.

6 Fold flaps out.

7 Rotate paper 90° clockwise, and turn paper over.

8 Fold edges in to center line.

32

9

Turn paper over.

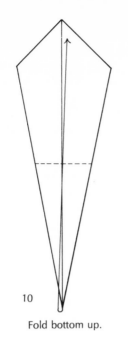

10

Fold bottom up.

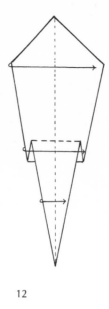

11

Fold top down ½″ from bottom.

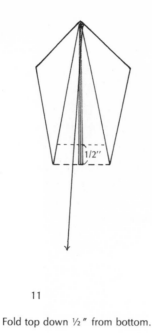

12

Fold paper in half.

13

Fold flap down.

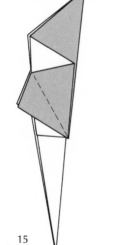

14

Turn paper over, and repeat step 13.

15

Turn paper over.

16

Hold flaps A and B tightly with thumb and index finger and hold abdomen with thumb and index finger. Push both sides up, sliding bottom of abdomen (shaded part) out.

17

Fold neck up two-thirds of the way from the end, creasing well.

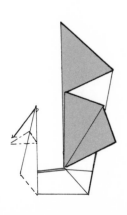

18

Fold head to the left, creasing well.

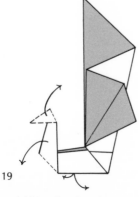

19

Unfold head and neck, and open sides of head, neck, and abdomen.

20

Fold neck back about 90° and head forward by the same amount, reversing creases, and fold sides of body together.

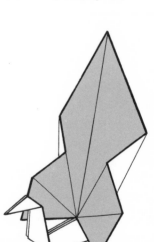

33

SWAN (3" high)

MATERIALS: 1 sheet of 6" × 6" paper

(see also pp. 124, 126, and 135 for suggested color, weight, and size)

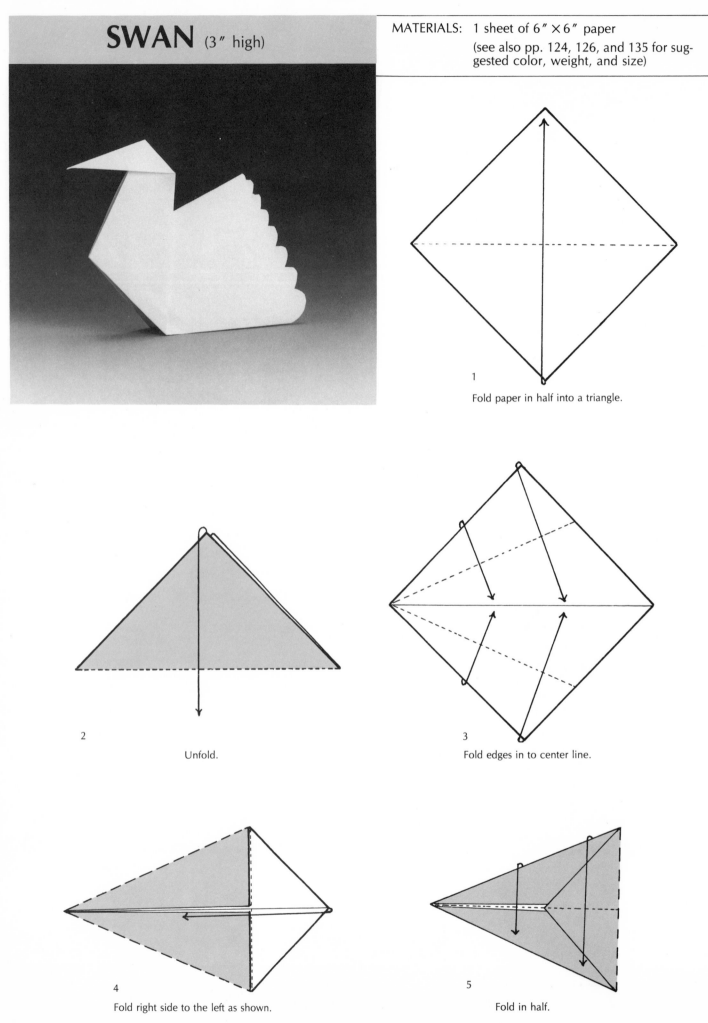

1

Fold paper in half into a triangle.

2

Unfold.

3

Fold edges in to center line.

4

Fold right side to the left as shown.

5

Fold in half.

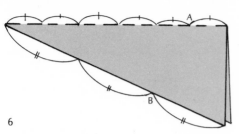

6

Divide bottom edge into three equal parts and top edge into six equal parts.

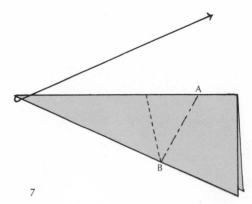

7

Fold neck on small dotted line so right edge is on line AB, creasing well.

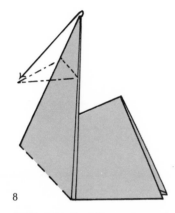

8

Fold head to the left, creasing well.

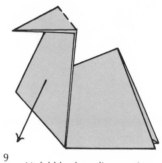

9

Unfold back to diagram 6.

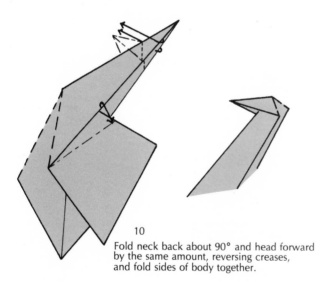

10

Fold neck back about 90° and head forward by the same amount, reversing creases, and fold sides of body together.

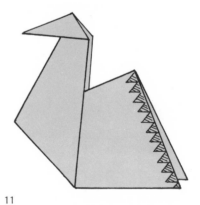

11

Cut the tail of the finished swan if you wish.

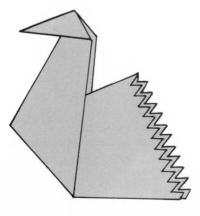

DOVE (5″ long)

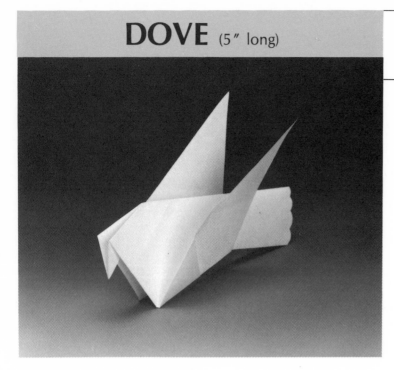

MATERIALS: 1 sheet of 6″ × 6″ paper

(see also pp. 124, 126, 131, and 137 for suggested color, weight, and size)

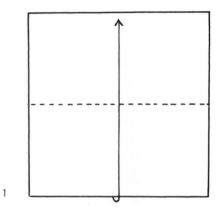

1

Fold paper in half into a rectangle.

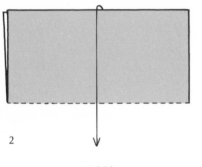

2

Unfold.

3

Fold two corners in to center.

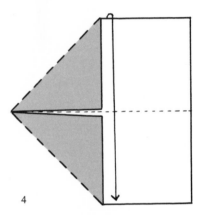

4

Fold paper in half.

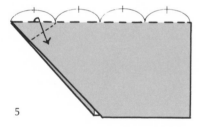

5

Fold head down to about 1½″ from edge, creasing well.

6

Fold head backwards on the same crease, again creasing well.

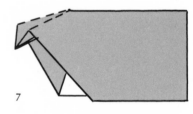

7

Return head to original position, and push top down, reversing the middle crease.

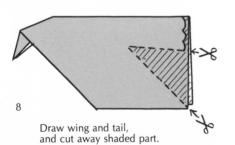

8

Draw wing and tail, and cut away shaded part.

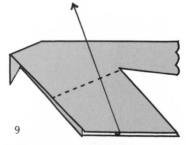

9

Fold wings up at slightly different angles so a bit of the other wing shows.

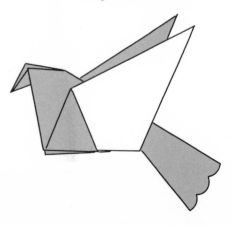

TREE (6½″ high)

MATERIALS: 1 sheet of 6″ × 6″ paper
(see also p. 124 and p. 126 for suggested color, weight, and size)
Glue

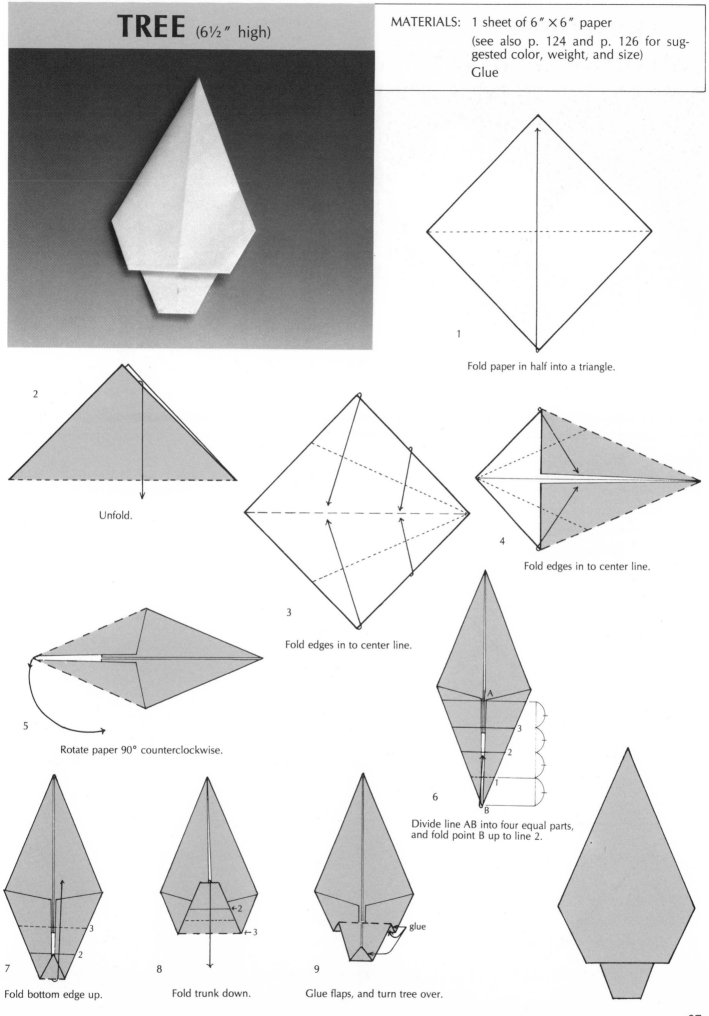

1

Fold paper in half into a triangle.

2

Unfold.

3

Fold edges in to center line.

4

Fold edges in to center line.

5

Rotate paper 90° counterclockwise.

6

Divide line AB into four equal parts, and fold point B up to line 2.

7

Fold bottom edge up.

8

Fold trunk down.

9

Glue flaps, and turn tree over.

glue

CARNATION (4″ wide)
MORNING GLORY (4″ wide)

MATERIALS: 1 sheet of 6″ × 6″ paper

(see also pp. 124, 126, and 147 for suggested color, weight, and size)

ATTENTION: Start with front or colored side of paper facing you.

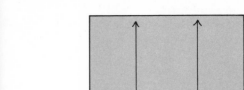

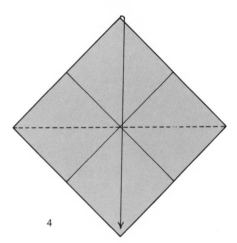

1 Fold paper in half into a rectangle, creasing well.

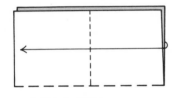

2 Fold in half into a square, creasing well.

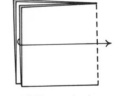

3 Unfold completely.

4 Fold paper in half into a triangle, creasing well.

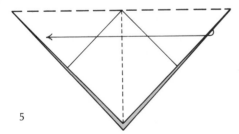

5 Fold in half into a triangle again, creasing well.

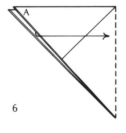

6 Hold point A (top layer) up straight from dotted line edge.

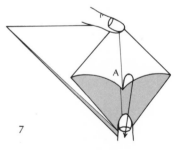

7 Open sides of this layer by sliding finger inside, and flatten into a diamond.

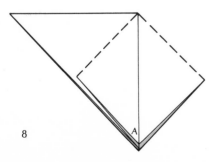

8 Turn paper over.

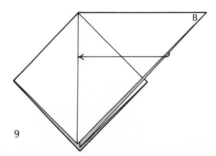

9 Hold point B up straight from crease.

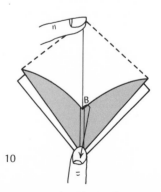

10 Open sides of point B by sliding finger inside, and flatten into a diamond.

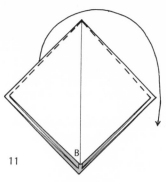

11

Rotate paper 180°.

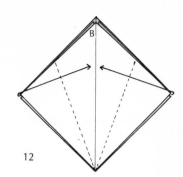

12

Fold top layer edges in to center line.

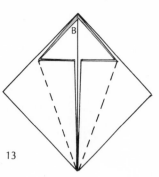

13

Turn paper over, and repeat step 12.

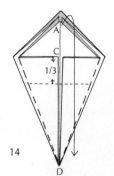

14

Fold point A (all layers) down about one-third the length of CD.

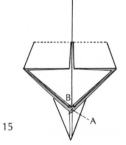

15

Pull point B up, holding point A down.

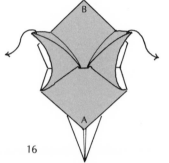

16

Open side triangles by sliding fingers inside, and flatten into diamonds.

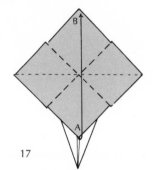

17

Fold point A up to point B.

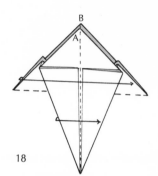

18

Fold left side (all layers) to the right.

19

Draw petals, and cut away shaded part.

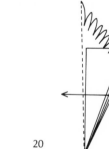

20

Fold right side back to the left.

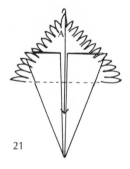

21

Fold point A back down.

MORNING GLORY:

Follow carnation steps 1–18, and then do the following steps.

19

Draw petals, and cut away shaded part.

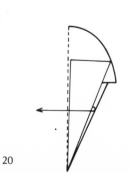

20

Fold right side back to the left.

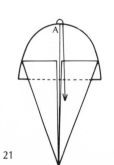

21

Fold point A back down.

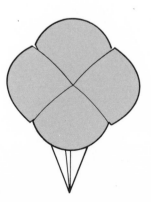

TULIP (4½″ wide)

MATERIALS: 1 sheet of 6″×6″ paper
(see also p. 124 and p. 126 for suggested color, weight, and size)

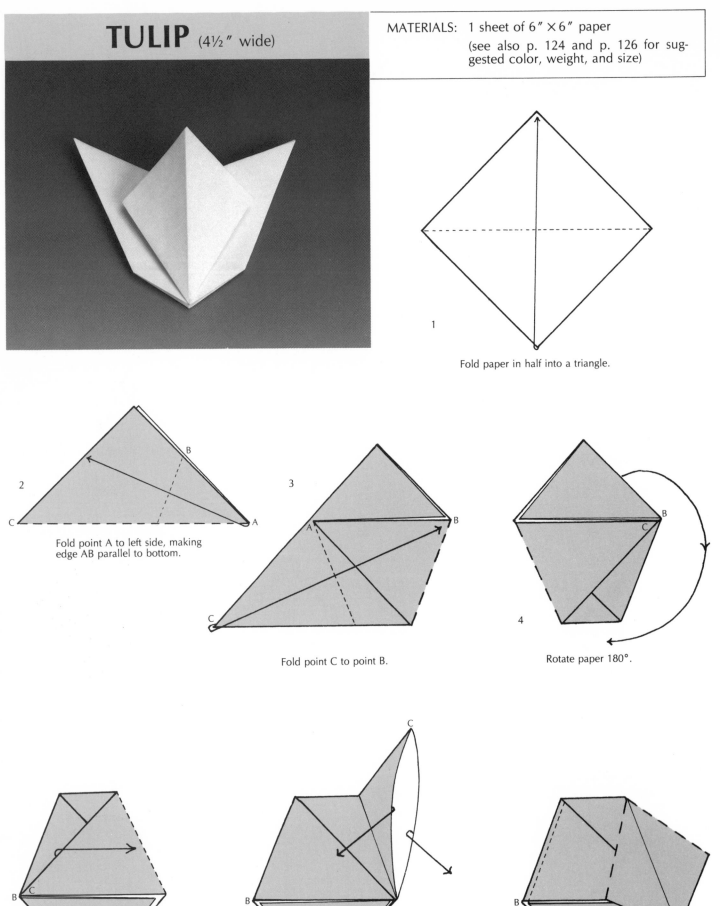

1 Fold paper in half into a triangle.

2 Fold point A to left side, making edge AB parallel to bottom.

3 Fold point C to point B.

4 Rotate paper 180°.

5 Hold point C straight up from edge.

6 Open sides by sliding finger inside, and flatten into a kite.

7 Repeat steps 5–6 with left side.

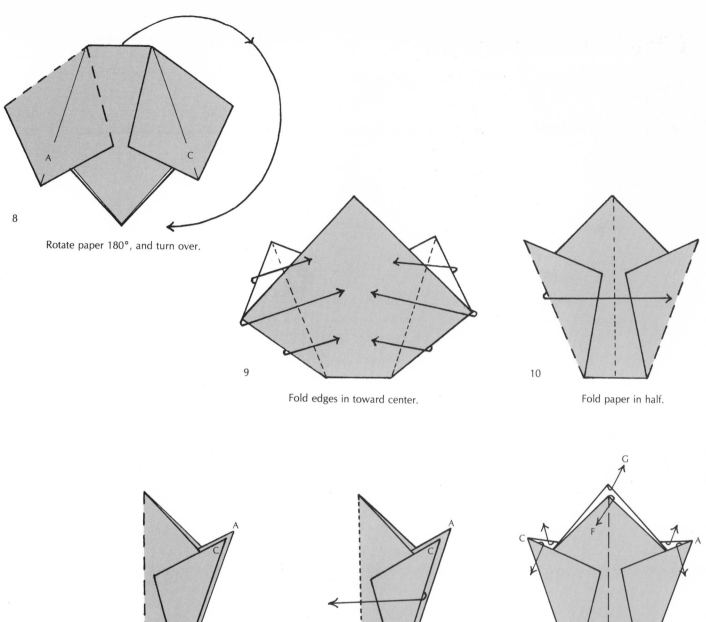

8

Rotate paper 180°, and turn over.

9

Fold edges in toward center.

10

Fold paper in half.

11

Fold point D to point E, creasing very well.

12

Unfold back to diagram 10.

13

Pull points F and G out, while pushing the sides in (A and C).

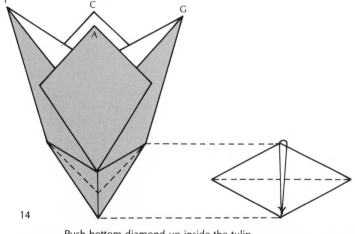

14

Push bottom diamond up inside the tulip, reversing the creases.

CHRYSANTHEMUM (3" wide)

MATERIALS: 1 sheet of 6" × 6" paper
(see also pp. 124, 126, 138, and 142 for
suggested color, weight, and size)
Glue

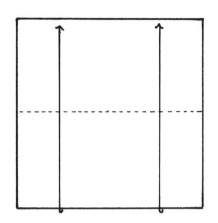

1

Fold paper in half into a rectangle.

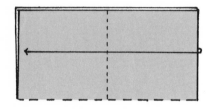

2

Fold in half into a square.

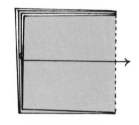

3

Unfold completely.

4

Fold edges in to center line.

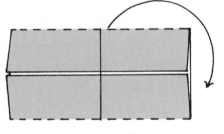

5

Rotate paper 90°.

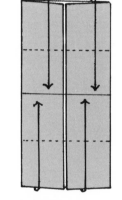

6

Fold edges in to center line.

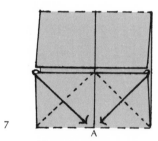

7

A

Fold corners down to point A.

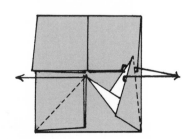

8

Pull top layer of each triangle out
to the side as far as it will go.

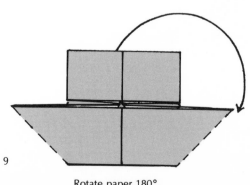

9

Rotate paper 180°,
and repeat steps 7–8.

42

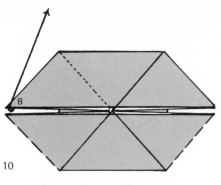

10

Hold point B up straight from crease.

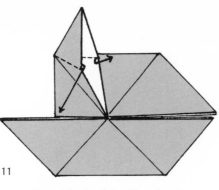

11

Open sides by sliding finger inside, and flatten into a square.

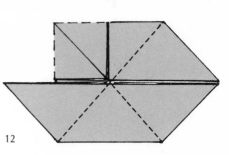

12

Repeat steps 10–11 with three other points.

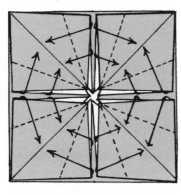

13

Fold edges of each small square in to center line.

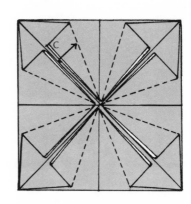

14

Hold point C straight up from crease.

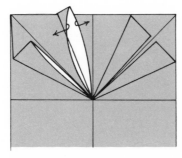

15

Open sides by sliding finger inside, and flatten into a kite.

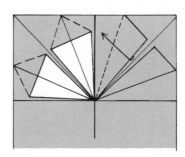

16

Repeat steps 14–15 with seven other points.

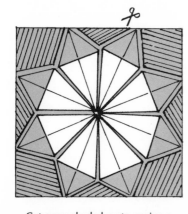

17

Cut away shaded parts, saving a scrap from one corner.

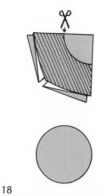

18

Cut the scrap along a curve as shown, open into circle, and glue it to the center.

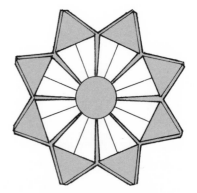

ROSE (3½″ wide)

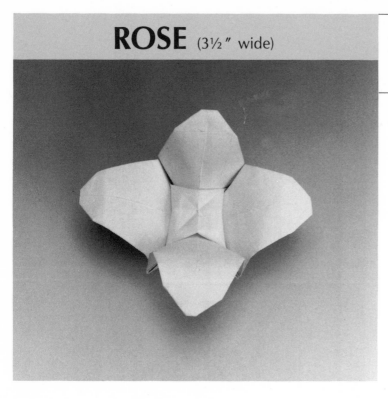

MATERIALS: 1 sheet of 6″ × 6″ paper
(see also pp. 124, 126, 144, and 147 for suggested color, weight, and size)
Glue

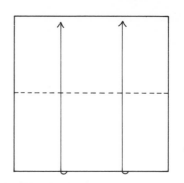

1

Fold paper in half into a rectangle, creasing well.

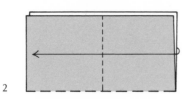

2

Fold in half into a square, creasing well.

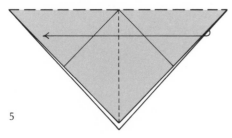

3

Unfold completely.

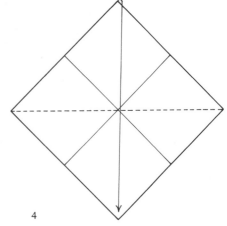

4

Fold paper in half into a triangle, creasing well.

5

Fold in half into a triangle again, creasing well.

6

Hold point A (top layer) up straight from dotted line edge.

7

Open sides of this layer by sliding finger inside, and flatten into a diamond.

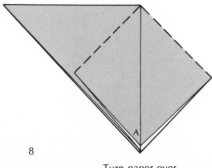

8

Turn paper over.

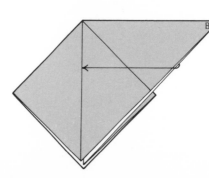

9

Hold point B up straight from crease.

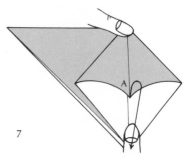

10

Open sides of point B by sliding finger inside, and flatten into a diamond.

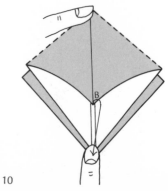

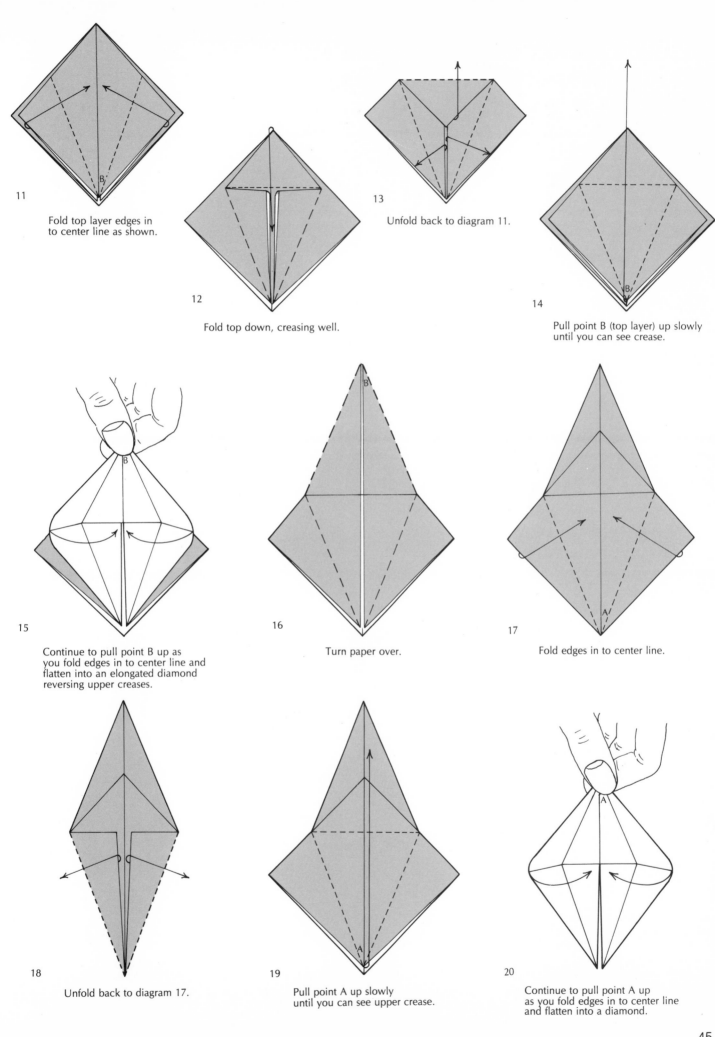

11 Fold top layer edges in to center line as shown.

12 Fold top down, creasing well.

13 Unfold back to diagram 11.

14 Pull point B (top layer) up slowly until you can see crease.

15 Continue to pull point B up as you fold edges in to center line and flatten into an elongated diamond reversing upper creases.

16 Turn paper over.

17 Fold edges in to center line.

18 Unfold back to diagram 17.

19 Pull point A up slowly until you can see upper crease.

20 Continue to pull point A up as you fold edges in to center line and flatten into a diamond.

45

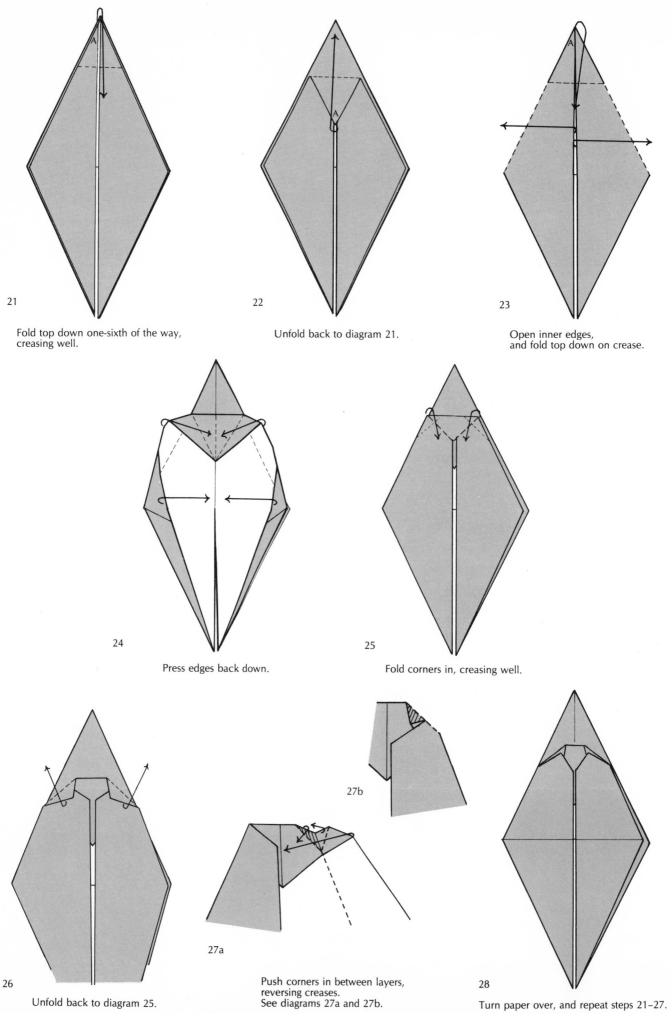

21

Fold top down one-sixth of the way, creasing well.

22

Unfold back to diagram 21.

23

Open inner edges, and fold top down on crease.

24

Press edges back down.

25

Fold corners in, creasing well.

26

Unfold back to diagram 25.

27a

27b

Push corners in between layers, reversing creases. See diagrams 27a and 27b.

28

Turn paper over, and repeat steps 21–27.

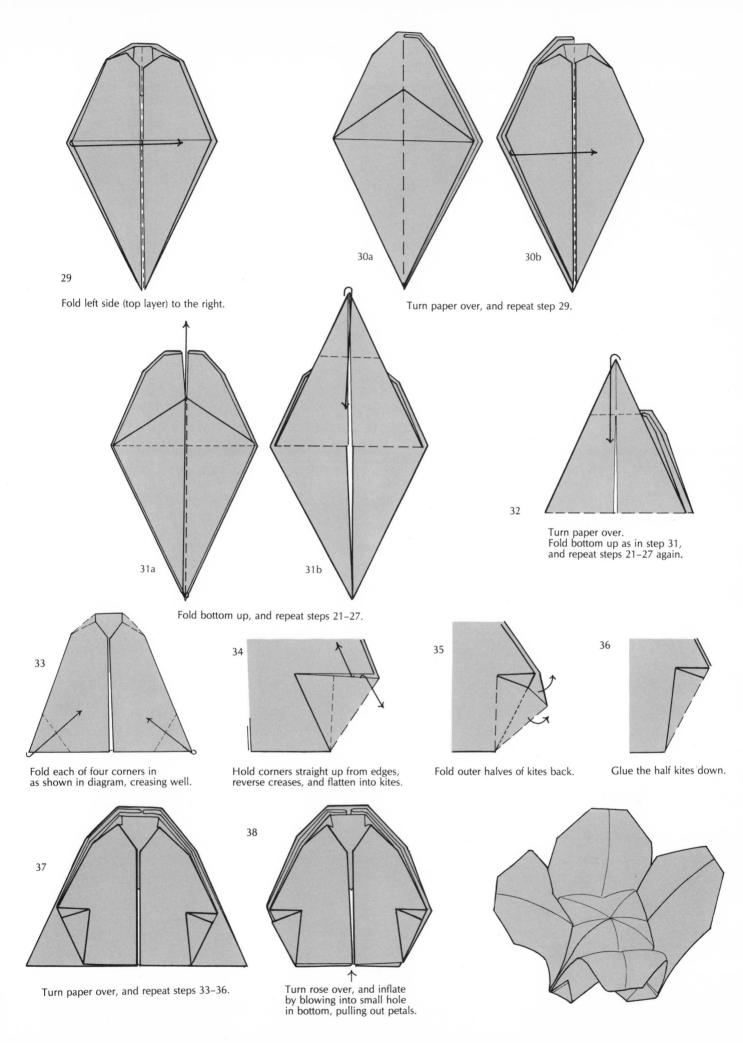

29

Fold left side (top layer) to the right.

30a

30b

Turn paper over, and repeat step 29.

31a

31b

Fold bottom up, and repeat steps 21–27.

32

Turn paper over.
Fold bottom up as in step 31,
and repeat steps 21–27 again.

33

Fold each of four corners in
as shown in diagram, creasing well.

34

Hold corners straight up from edges,
reverse creases, and flatten into kites.

35

Fold outer halves of kites back.

36

Glue the half kites down.

37

Turn paper over, and repeat steps 33–36.

38

Turn rose over, and inflate
by blowing into small hole
in bottom, pulling out petals.

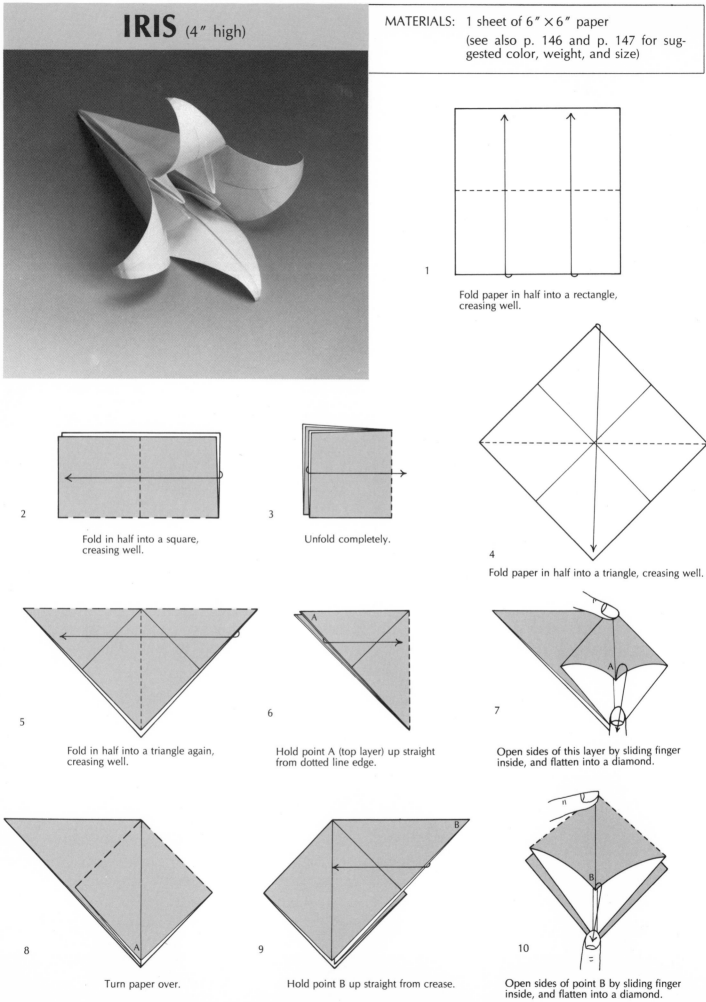

IRIS (4" high)

MATERIALS: 1 sheet of 6" × 6" paper
(see also p. 146 and p. 147 for suggested color, weight, and size)

1 Fold paper in half into a rectangle, creasing well.

2 Fold in half into a square, creasing well.

3 Unfold completely.

4 Fold paper in half into a triangle, creasing well.

5 Fold in half into a triangle again, creasing well.

6 Hold point A (top layer) up straight from dotted line edge.

7 Open sides of this layer by sliding finger inside, and flatten into a diamond.

8 Turn paper over.

9 Hold point B up straight from crease.

10 Open sides of point B by sliding finger inside, and flatten into a diamond.

48

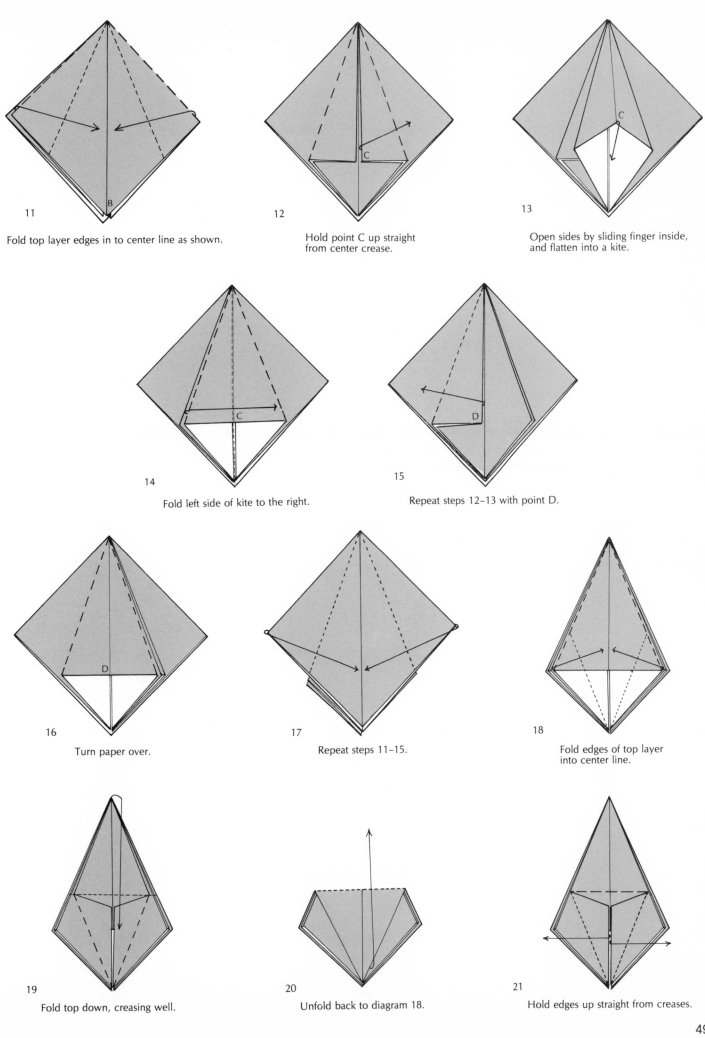

11

Fold top layer edges in to center line as shown.

12

Hold point C up straight from center crease.

13

Open sides by sliding finger inside, and flatten into a kite.

14

Fold left side of kite to the right.

15

Repeat steps 12–13 with point D.

16

Turn paper over.

17

Repeat steps 11–15.

18

Fold edges of top layer into center line.

19

Fold top down, creasing well.

20

Unfold back to diagram 18.

21

Hold edges up straight from creases.

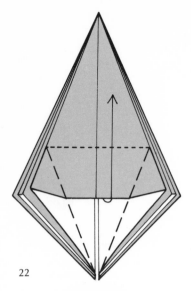

22

Pull flap up slowly until
you can see the crease.

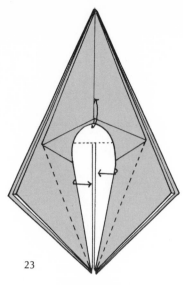

23

Continue to pull flap up as
you fold edges in to center
line, and flatten into a kite.

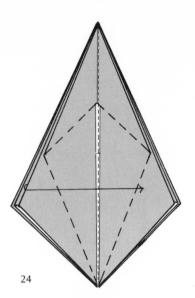

24

Fold two left layers to the right,
and repeat steps 18–23.

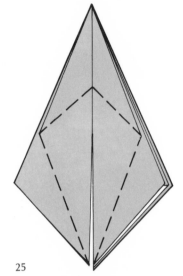

25

Turn paper over,
and repeat steps 18–23.

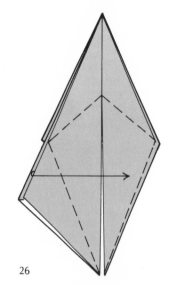

26

Fold two left layers to the right
and repeat steps 18–23.

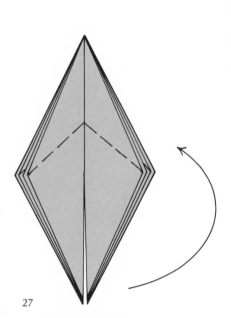

27

Rotate paper 180°

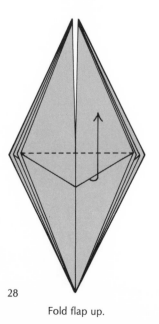

28

Fold flap up.

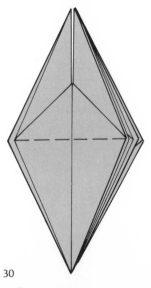

29

Fold two left layers
to the right, and fold flap up.

30

Turn paper over,
and repeat steps 28–29.

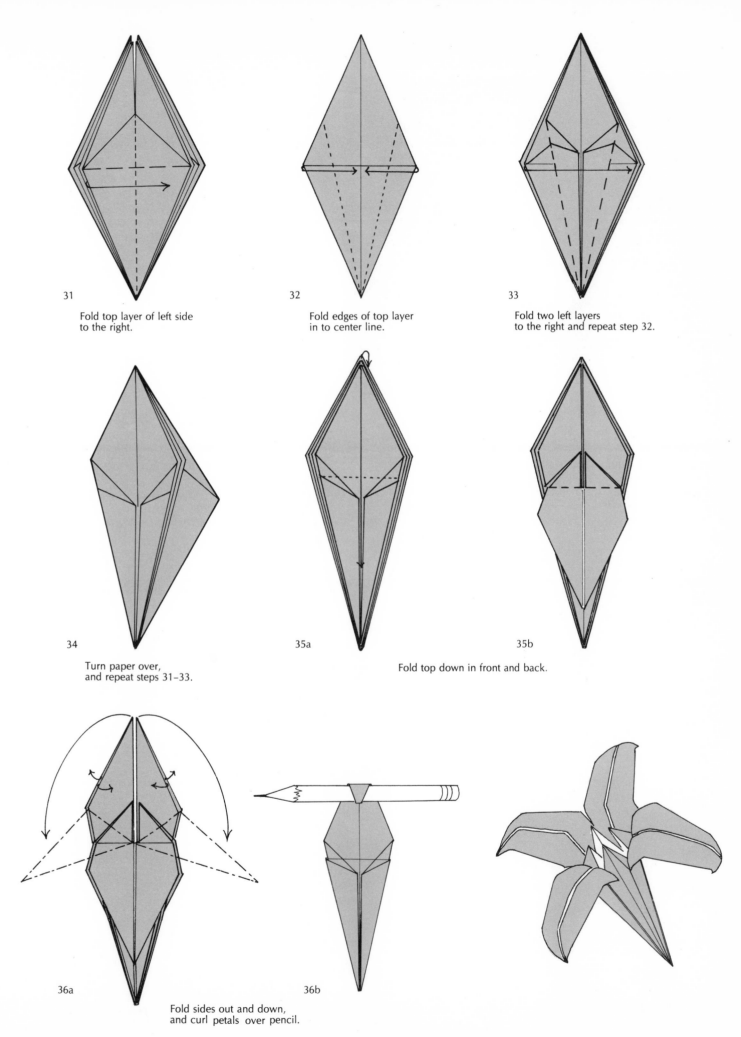

31
Fold top layer of left side
to the right.

32
Fold edges of top layer
in to center line.

33
Fold two left layers
to the right and repeat step 32.

34
Turn paper over,
and repeat steps 31–33.

35a

35b
Fold top down in front and back.

36a

36b
Fold sides out and down,
and curl petals over pencil.

PERSIMMON (2¼″ wide)

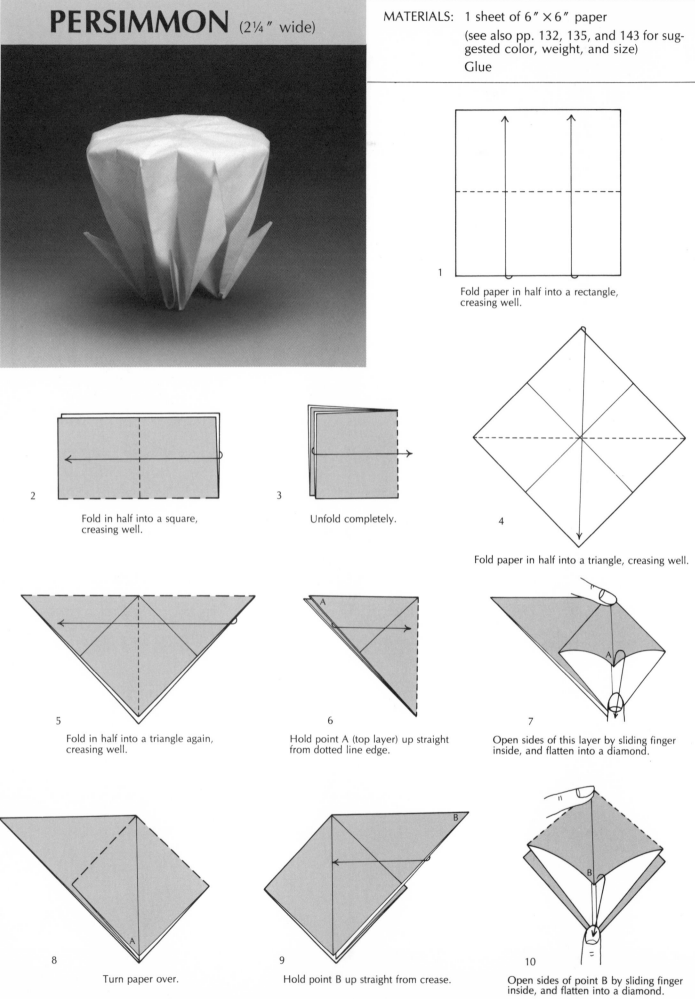

MATERIALS: 1 sheet of 6″ × 6″ paper
(see also pp. 132, 135, and 143 for suggested color, weight, and size)
Glue

1 Fold paper in half into a rectangle, creasing well.

2 Fold in half into a square, creasing well.

3 Unfold completely.

4 Fold paper in half into a triangle, creasing well.

5 Fold in half into a triangle again, creasing well.

6 Hold point A (top layer) up straight from dotted line edge.

7 Open sides of this layer by sliding finger inside, and flatten into a diamond.

8 Turn paper over.

9 Hold point B up straight from crease.

10 Open sides of point B by sliding finger inside, and flatten into a diamond.

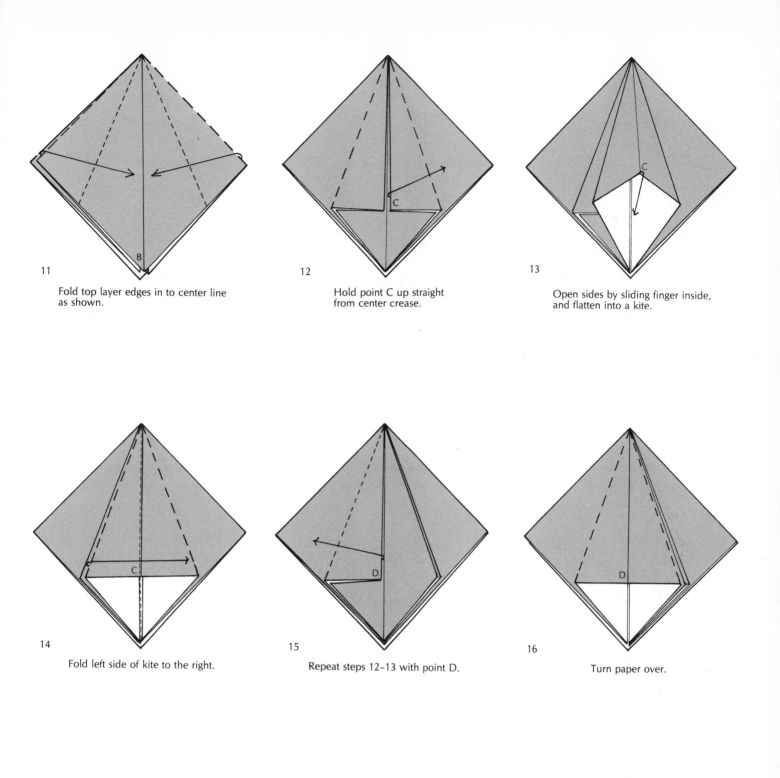

11

Fold top layer edges in to center line
as shown.

12

Hold point C up straight
from center crease.

13

Open sides by sliding finger inside,
and flatten into a kite.

14

Fold left side of kite to the right.

15

Repeat steps 12-13 with point D.

16

Turn paper over.

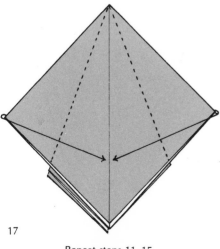

17

Repeat steps 11-15.

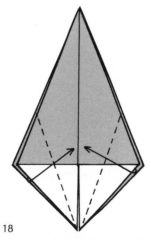

18

Fold lower edges of top layer
in to center line.

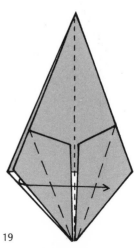

19

Fold two left layers to the right,
and repeat step 18.

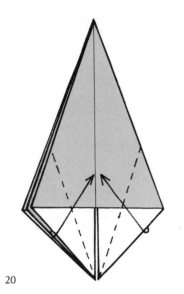

20

Turn paper over,
and repeat steps 18–19.

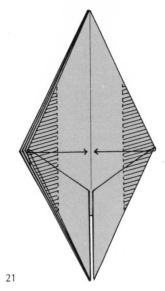

21

Apply glue to shaded areas
and fold corners of top layer
in to center line.

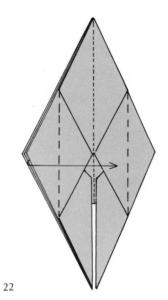

22

Fold two left layers to the right,
and repeat step 21.

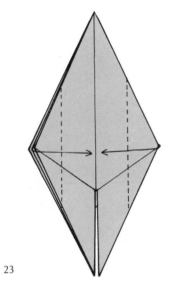

23

Turn paper over, and repeat steps 21–22.

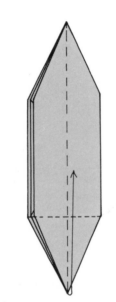

24

Fold top layer of left side to the right,
and fold bottom point up.

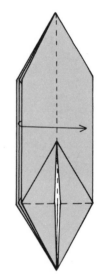

25

Fold two left layers to the right,
and fold bottom point up.

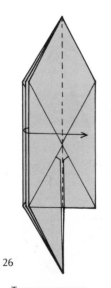

26

Turn paper over,
and repeat steps 24–25.

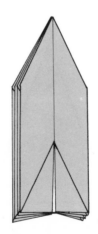

27

Blow into opening in bottom
to inflate persimmon, pushing upper
sides out from inside, if necessary.

54

CAMELLIA (3″ wide)

MATERIALS: 1 sheet of 6″ × 6″ paper
(see also p. 144 for suggested color, weight, and size)

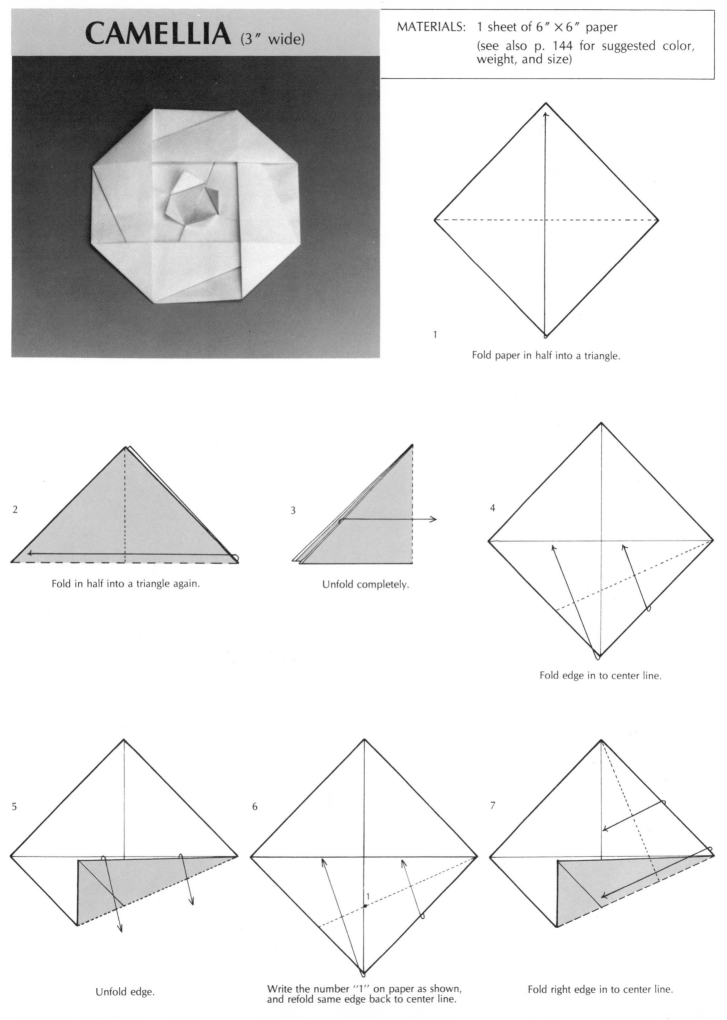

1 Fold paper in half into a triangle.

2 Fold in half into a triangle again.

3 Unfold completely.

4 Fold edge in to center line.

5 Unfold edge.

6 Write the number "1" on paper as shown, and refold same edge back to center line.

7 Fold right edge in to center line.

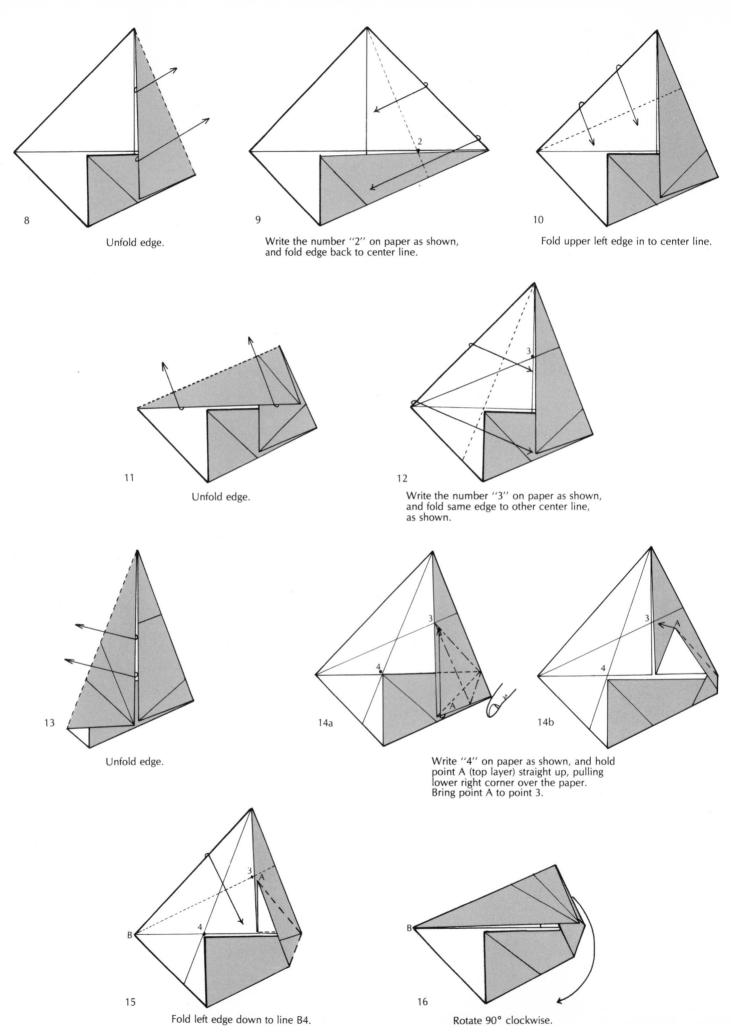

8   Unfold edge.

9   Write the number "2" on paper as shown, and fold edge back to center line.

10   Fold upper left edge in to center line.

11   Unfold edge.

12   Write the number "3" on paper as shown, and fold same edge to other center line, as shown.

13   Unfold edge.

14a

14b   Write "4" on paper as shown, and hold point A (top layer) straight up, pulling lower right corner over the paper. Bring point A to point 3.

15   Fold left edge down to line B4.

16   Rotate 90° clockwise.

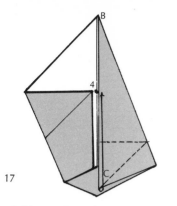

17

Fold point C (top layer) up to point 4, proceeding as in step 14.

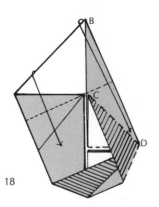

18

Fold point B down to point D.

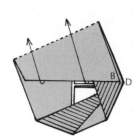

19

Unfold to diagram 18.

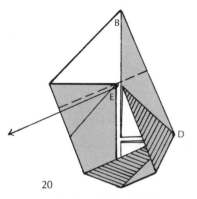

20

Pull point E to the left until you can see point 1.

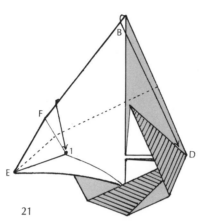

21

Fold point B to point D making a long crease to point E. (Point F should meet point 1.)

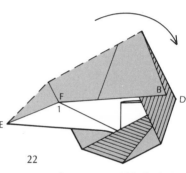

22

Rotate paper 90° clockwise.

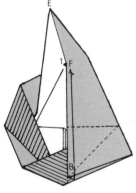

23

Fold point B up to point F (1), proceeding as in step 14.

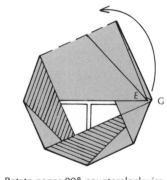

24

Fold point E down to point G.

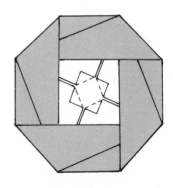

25

Rotate paper 90° counterclockwise.

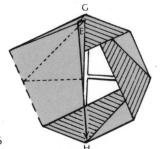

26

Fold point E to point H, proceeding as in step 14.

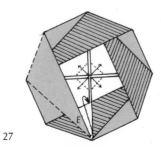

27

Slip point E under triangle, and fold back center flaps.

POINSETTIA (3¼″ wide)

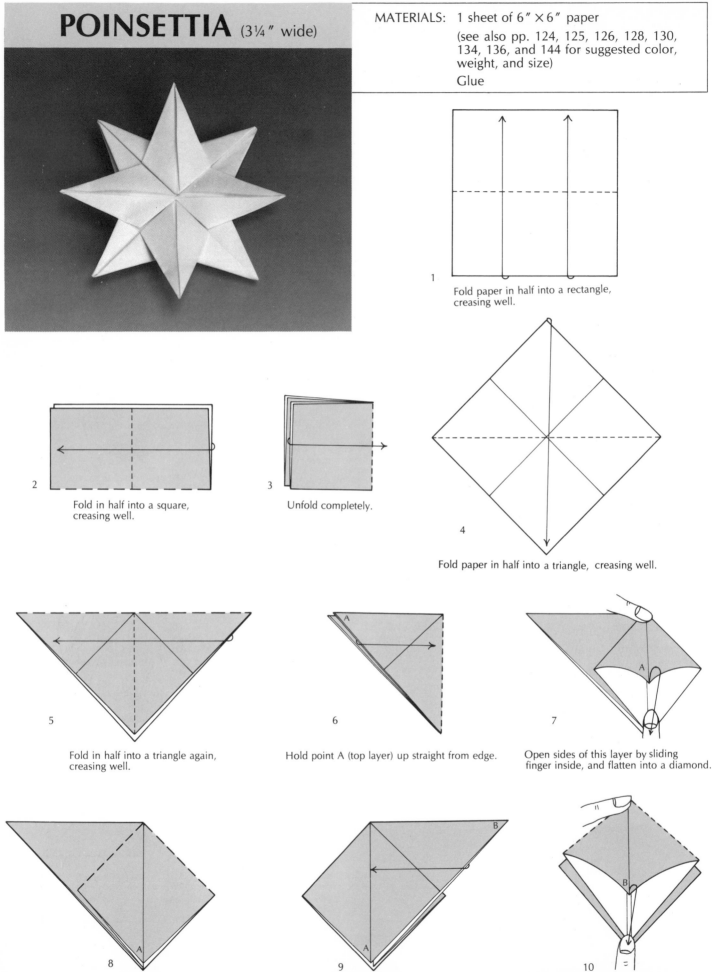

MATERIALS: 1 sheet of 6″ × 6″ paper
(see also pp. 124, 125, 126, 128, 130, 134, 136, and 144 for suggested color, weight, and size)
Glue

1 Fold paper in half into a rectangle, creasing well.

2 Fold in half into a square, creasing well.

3 Unfold completely.

4 Fold paper in half into a triangle, creasing well.

5 Fold in half into a triangle again, creasing well.

6 Hold point A (top layer) up straight from edge.

7 Open sides of this layer by sliding finger inside, and flatten into a diamond.

8 Turn paper over.

9 Hold point B up straight from crease.

10 Open sides of point B by sliding finger inside, and flatten into a diamond.

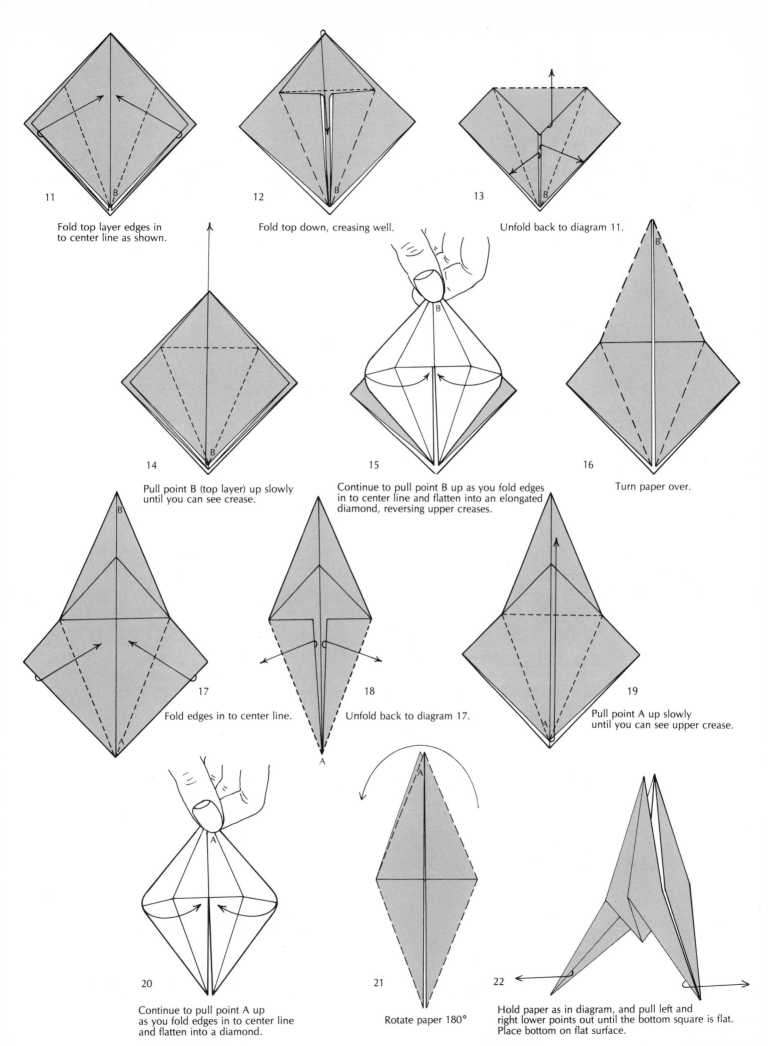

11 Fold top layer edges in to center line as shown.

12 Fold top down, creasing well.

13 Unfold back to diagram 11.

14 Pull point B (top layer) up slowly until you can see crease.

15 Continue to pull point B up as you fold edges in to center line and flatten into an elongated diamond, reversing upper creases.

16 Turn paper over.

17 Fold edges in to center line.

18 Unfold back to diagram 17.

19 Pull point A up slowly until you can see upper crease.

20 Continue to pull point A up as you fold edges in to center line and flatten into a diamond.

21 Rotate paper 180°

22 Hold paper as in diagram, and pull left and right lower points out until the bottom square is flat. Place bottom on flat surface.

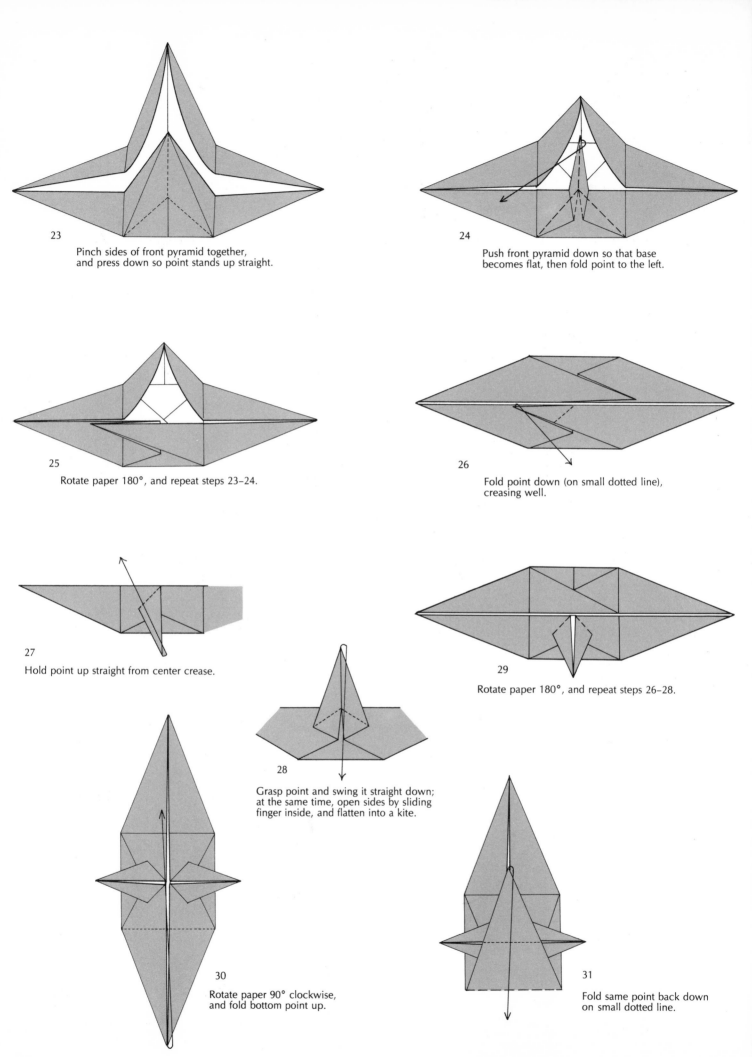

23
Pinch sides of front pyramid together,
and press down so point stands up straight.

24
Push front pyramid down so that base
becomes flat, then fold point to the left.

25
Rotate paper 180°, and repeat steps 23–24.

26
Fold point down (on small dotted line),
creasing well.

27
Hold point up straight from center crease.

28
Grasp point and swing it straight down;
at the same time, open sides by sliding
finger inside, and flatten into a kite.

29
Rotate paper 180°, and repeat steps 26–28.

30
Rotate paper 90° clockwise,
and fold bottom point up.

31
Fold same point back down
on small dotted line.

60

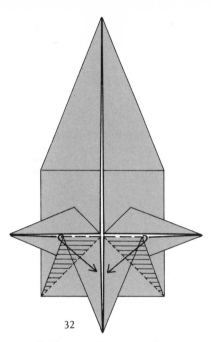

32

Fold corners in to center line, creasing well.

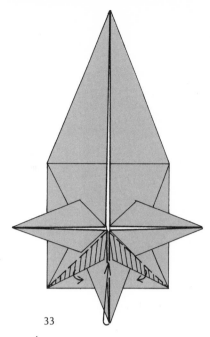

33

Pull bottom point out, and push shaded triangles in back of kite, reversing creases.

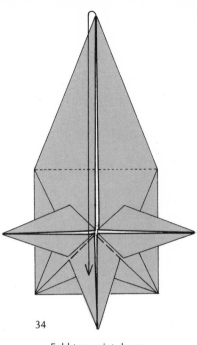

34

Fold top point down.

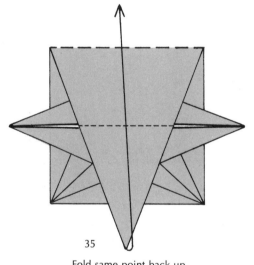

35

Fold same point back up.

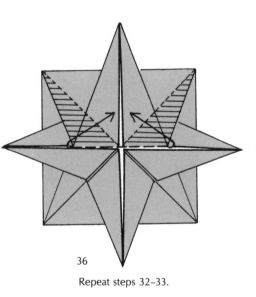

36

Repeat steps 32–33.

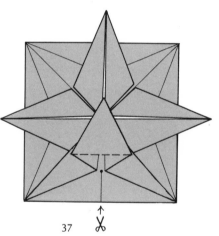

37 ✂

Hold bottom point up straight, and cut from edge to fold.

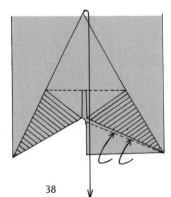

38

Fold flaps under shaded areas, and glue them.

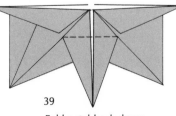

39

Fold petal back down.

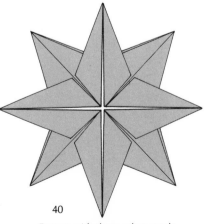

40

Repeat with three other petals, and glue them in place.

SANTA CLAUS (4" high)

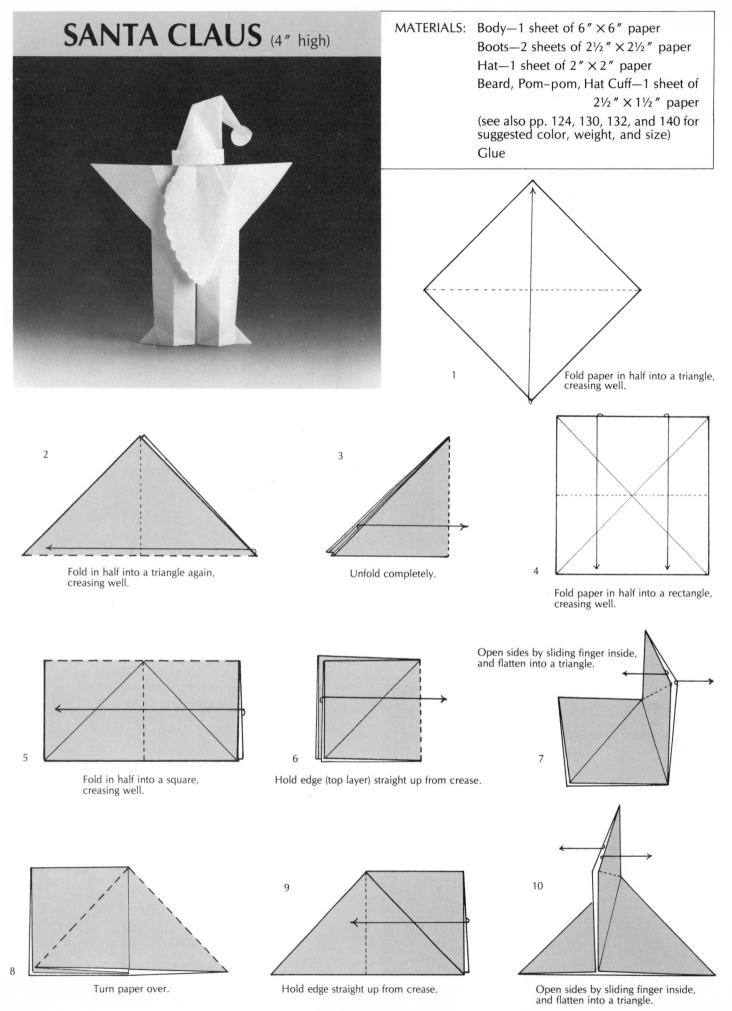

MATERIALS: Body—1 sheet of 6″ × 6″ paper
Boots—2 sheets of 2½″ × 2½″ paper
Hat—1 sheet of 2″ × 2″ paper
Beard, Pom–pom, Hat Cuff—1 sheet of
2½″ × 1½″ paper
(see also pp. 124, 130, 132, and 140 for
suggested color, weight, and size)
Glue

1 Fold paper in half into a triangle, creasing well.

2 Fold in half into a triangle again, creasing well.

3 Unfold completely.

4 Fold paper in half into a rectangle, creasing well.

5 Fold in half into a square, creasing well.

6 Hold edge (top layer) straight up from crease.

7 Open sides by sliding finger inside, and flatten into a triangle.

8 Turn paper over.

9 Hold edge straight up from crease.

10 Open sides by sliding finger inside, and flatten into a triangle.

62

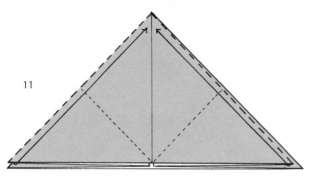

11

Fold corners (top layers) in to center line.

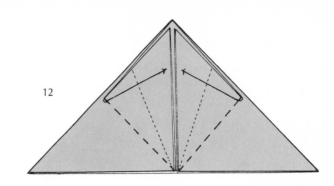

12

Fold edges in to center line.

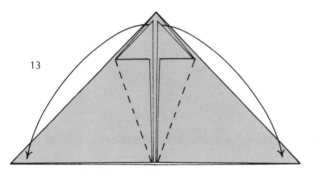

13

Unfold back to diagram 11.

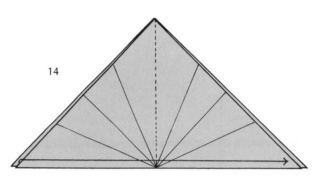

14

Fold left side (top layer) to the right.

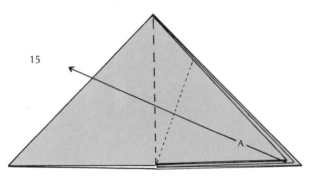

15

Fold point A to the left.

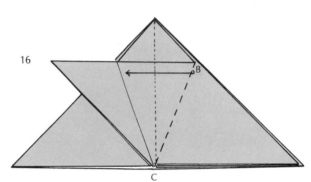

16

Fold edge BC to the left.

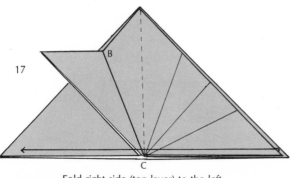

17

Fold right side (top layer) to the left.

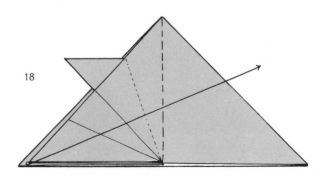

18

Repeat steps 15 and 16 with left side, reversing directions accordingly.

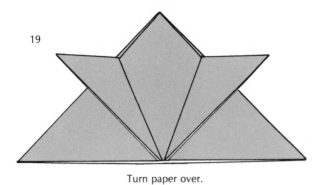

19

Turn paper over.

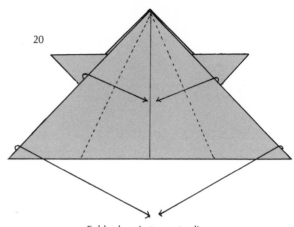

20

Fold edges in to center line.

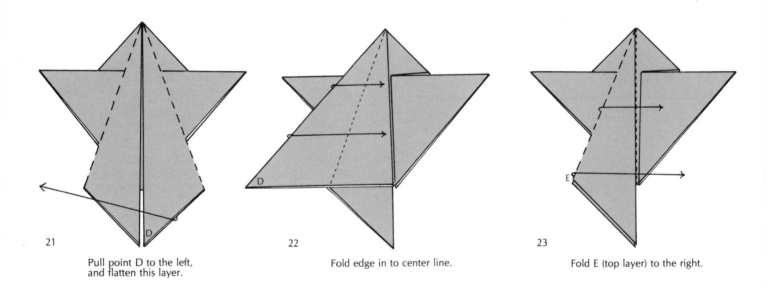

21

Pull point D to the left,
and flatten this layer.

22

Fold edge in to center line.

23

Fold E (top layer) to the right.

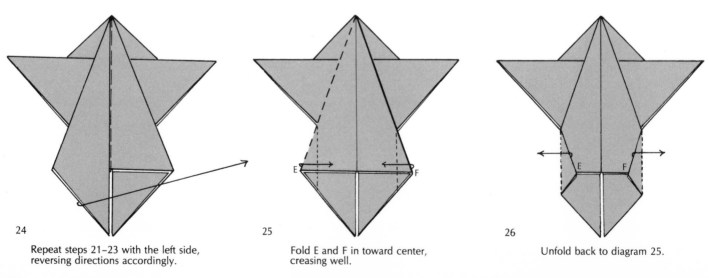

24

Repeat steps 21–23 with the left side,
reversing directions accordingly.

25

Fold E and F in toward center,
creasing well.

26

Unfold back to diagram 25.

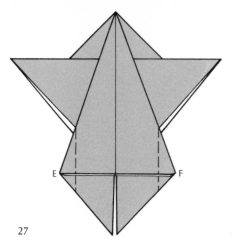

27

Push E and F between top and bottom layers, reversing the creases.

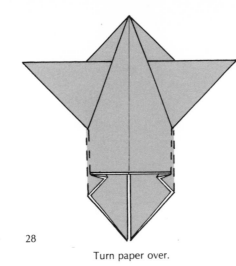

28

Turn paper over.

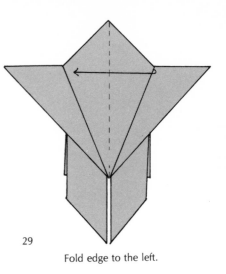

29

Fold edge to the left.

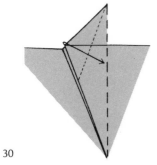

30

Fold edge in to center line.

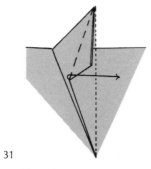

31

Fold this layer to the right.

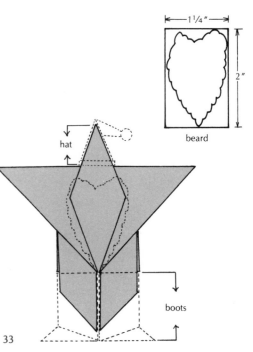

1¼"

2"

beard

hat

boots

33

Cut Santa's beard out and glue it on his face. Then make his boots and hat and glue them on.

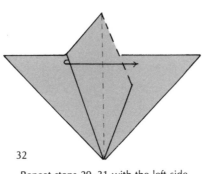

32

Repeat steps 29–31 with the left side, reversing directions accordingly.

LEFT BOOT:

ATTENTION: Start with front or colored side of paper facing you.

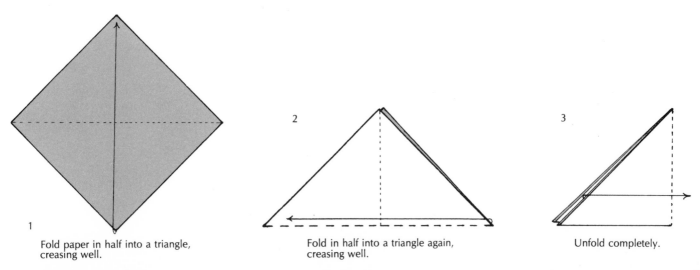

1

Fold paper in half into a triangle, creasing well.

2

Fold in half into a triangle again, creasing well.

3

Unfold completely.

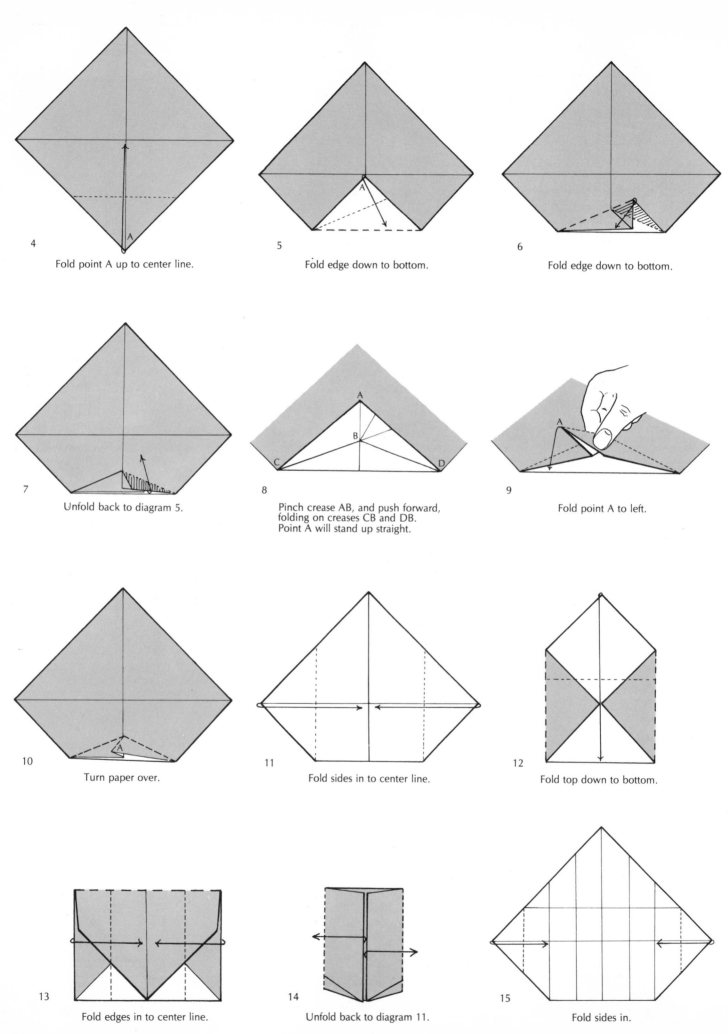

4

Fold point A up to center line.

5

Fold edge down to bottom.

6

Fold edge down to bottom.

7

Unfold back to diagram 5.

8

Pinch crease AB, and push forward,
folding on creases CB and DB.
Point A will stand up straight.

9

Fold point A to left.

10

Turn paper over.

11

Fold sides in to center line.

12

Fold top down to bottom.

13

Fold edges in to center line.

14

Unfold back to diagram 11.

15

Fold sides in.

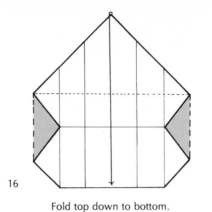

16

Fold top down to bottom.

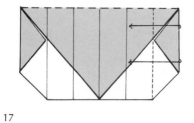

17

Fold right edge in.

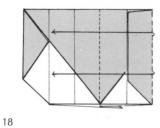

18

Fold right edge in again.

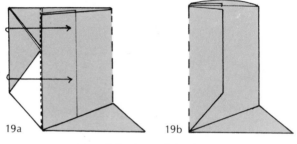

19a   19b

Put a little glue on left side,
and fold left edge to the right,
pressing together.

RIGHT BOOT:

1–16   Follow directions for Left Boot, steps 1–16.

17   Fold left edge in.

18   Fold left edge in again.

19   Put a little glue on right side,
and fold right side to the left,
pressing together.

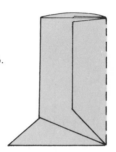

HAT:

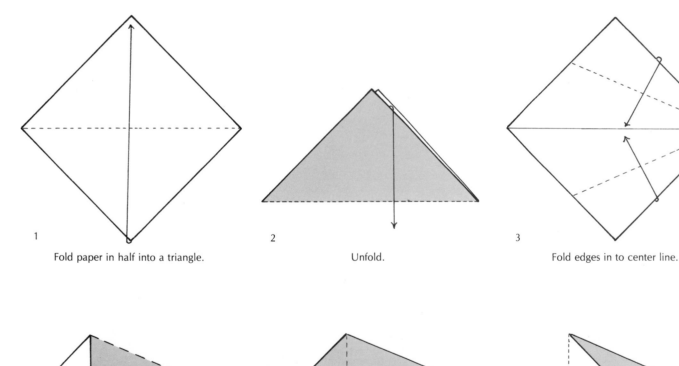

1

Fold paper in half into a triangle.

2

Unfold.

3

Fold edges in to center line.

4

Turn paper over.

5

Fold point A to the right.

6

Unfold back to diagram 5.

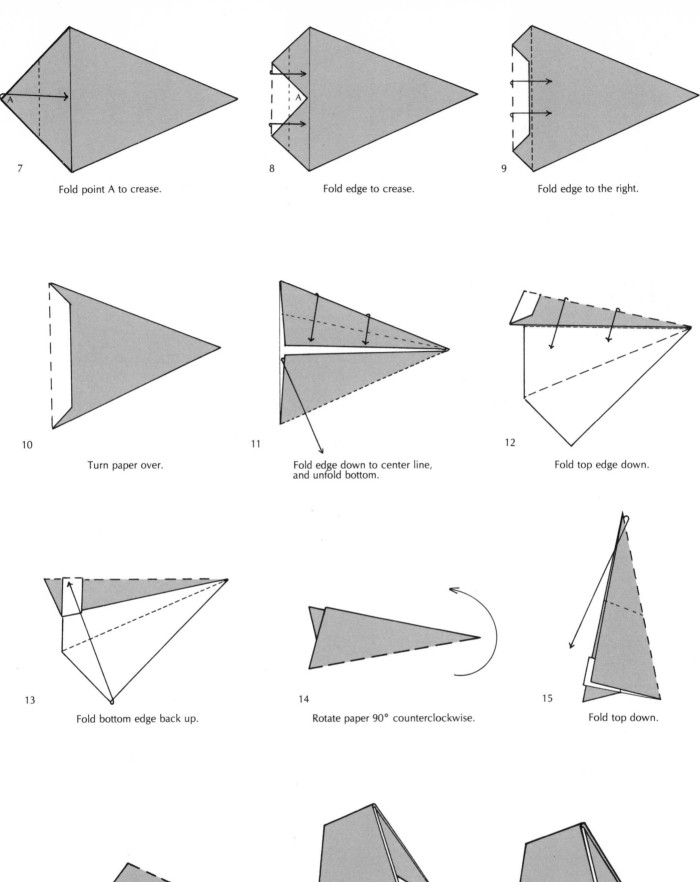

7 Fold point A to crease.

8 Fold edge to crease.

9 Fold edge to the right.

10 Turn paper over.

11 Fold edge down to center line, and unfold bottom.

12 Fold top edge down.

13 Fold bottom edge back up.

14 Rotate paper 90° counterclockwise.

15 Fold top down.

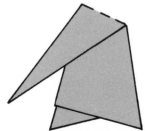

16 Glue flap, and turn hat over.

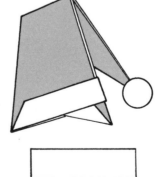

17 Cut ¼″ diameter circle and glue it on top of the hat. Cut ¼″ × ¾″ strip of paper and glue it to the hat's cuff.

MARY/NUN (3¾″ high)

MATERIALS: 1 sheet of 6″ × 6″ paper
(see also p. 128 and p. 148 for suggested color, weight, and size)
Glue or stapler

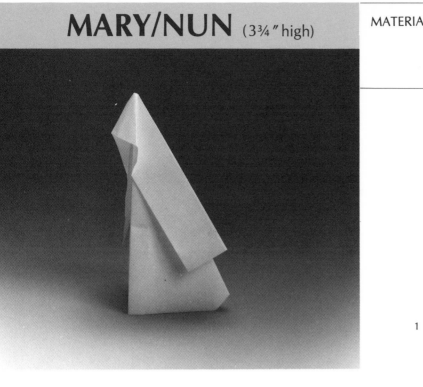

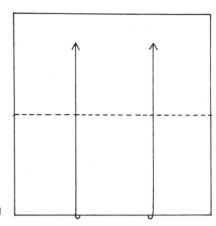

1 Fold paper in half into a rectangle, creasing well.

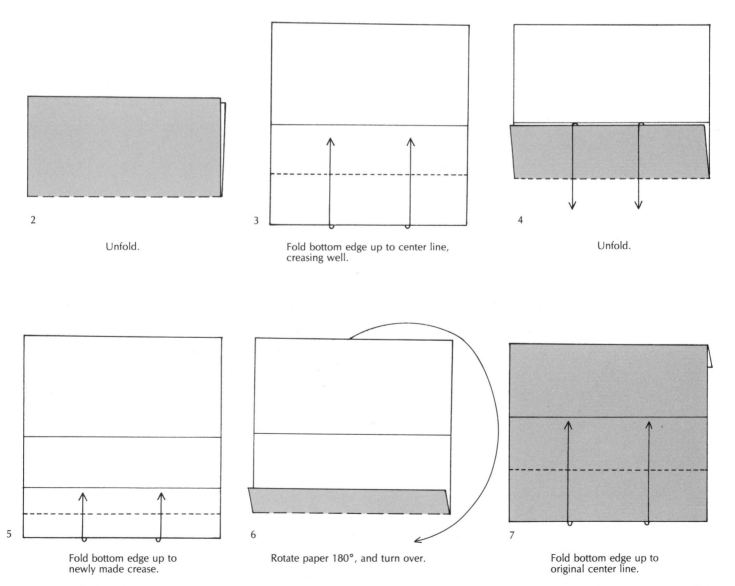

2 Unfold.

3 Fold bottom edge up to center line, creasing well.

4 Unfold.

5 Fold bottom edge up to newly made crease.

6 Rotate paper 180°, and turn over.

7 Fold bottom edge up to original center line.

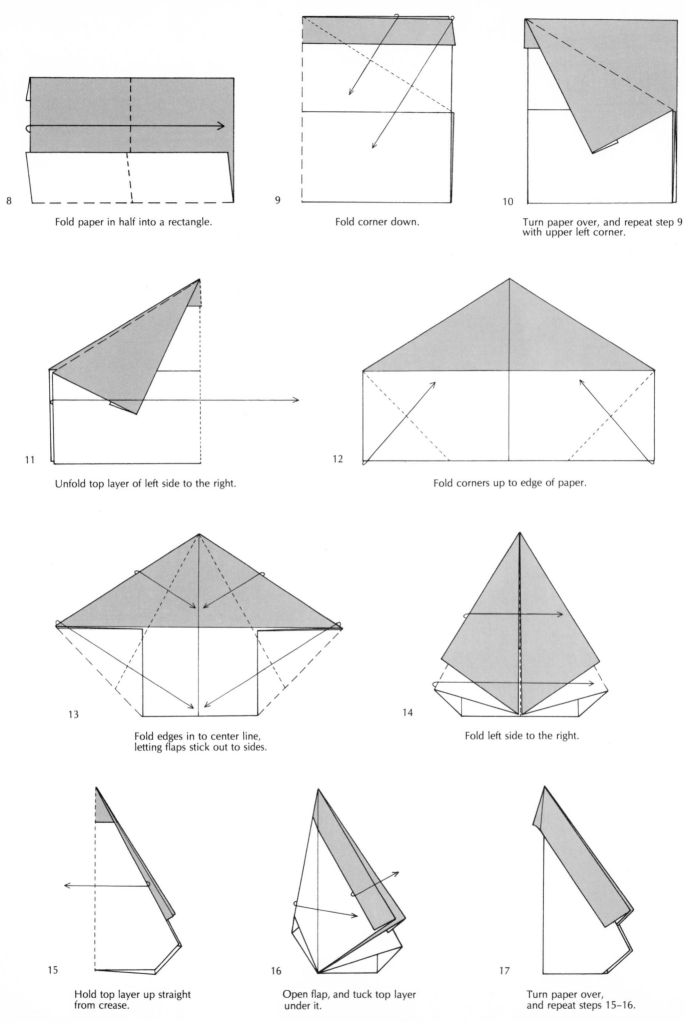

8

Fold paper in half into a rectangle.

9

Fold corner down.

10

Turn paper over, and repeat step 9 with upper left corner.

11

Unfold top layer of left side to the right.

12

Fold corners up to edge of paper.

13

Fold edges in to center line, letting flaps stick out to sides.

14

Fold left side to the right.

15

Hold top layer up straight from crease.

16

Open flap, and tuck top layer under it.

17

Turn paper over, and repeat steps 15–16.

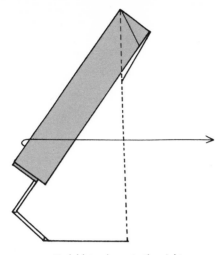

18

Unfold top layer to the right.

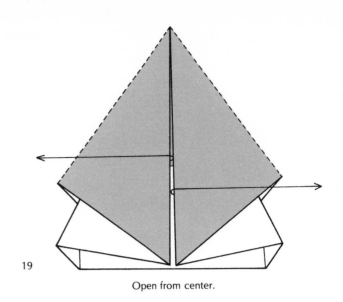

19

Open from center.

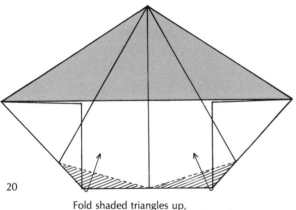

20

Fold shaded triangles up,
creasing well, to round hemline.

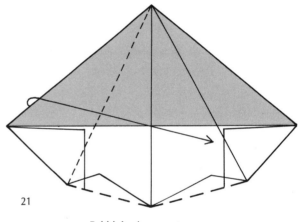

21

Fold left edge over to crease.

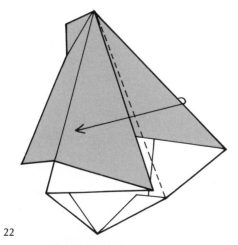

22

Fold right edge over to crease.

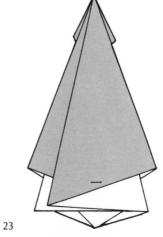

23

Glue or staple.

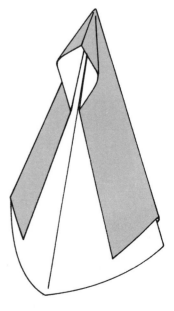

INFANT JESUS (4¾″ high)

MATERIALS: 1 sheet of 6″ × 6″ paper

(see also p. 128 for suggested color, weight, and size)

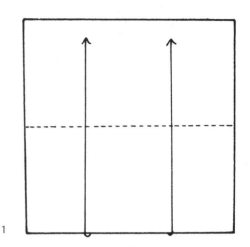

1

Fold paper in half into a rectangle, creasing well.

2

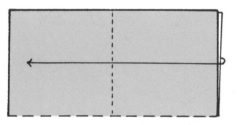

Fold in half into a square, creasing well.

3

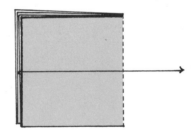

Unfold back to diagram 2.

4

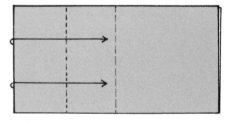

Fold left edge in to center line, creasing well.

5

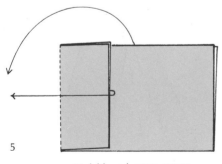

Unfold, and rotate paper 90° counterclockwise.

6

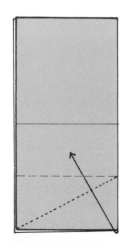

Fold corner up creasing well.

7

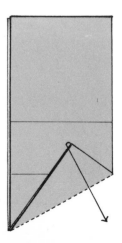

Unfold back to diagram 6, and rotate paper 180°.

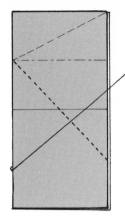

8

Fold left edge up to crease,
creasing well.

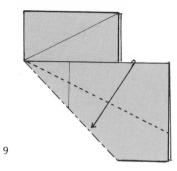

9

Fold edge back down to newly made crease,
creasing well.

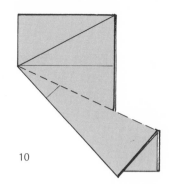

10

Unfold completely. (Colored side
of paper should be facing down,
as in step 1.)

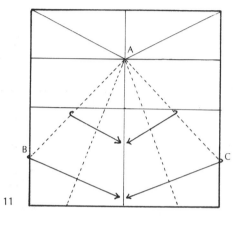

11

Fold crease AC in to center line.
(Flap goes underneath fold.)

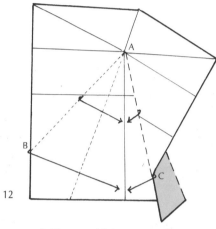

12

Fold crease AB in to center line.
(Flap goes underneath fold.)

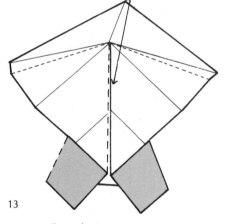

13

Press down top into
nearly triangular shape.
You won't quite be able
to use existing creases.

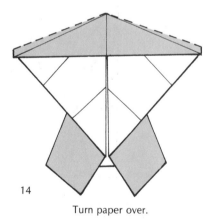

14

Turn paper over.

15

Fold edges of bottom flaps in
almost to center line,
creasing well, to make feet.

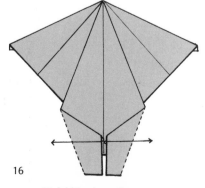

16

Unfold back to diagram 15.

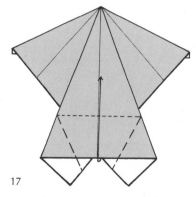

17

Fold bottom up, creasing well.

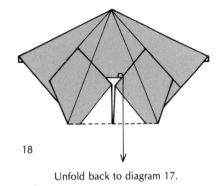

18

Unfold back to diagram 17.

19

Push top layer of paper up,
fold edges inside, reversing creases,
and press flat.

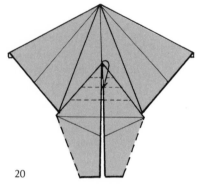

20

Fold top of triangle down one-quarter
of the way, then fold down same amount
twice more.

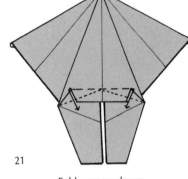

21

Fold corners down,
and turn paper over.

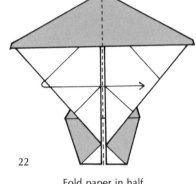

22

Fold paper in half.

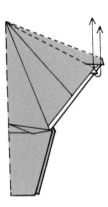

23

Pull top flap out.

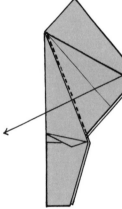

24

Fold top right flap edge
toward you and to the left,
creasing well.

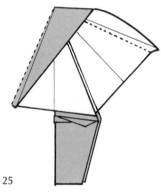

25

Turn paper over.

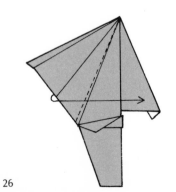

26

Fold left flap edge to the right,
creasing well, and turn paper over.

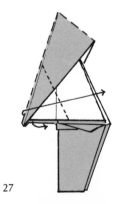

27

Fold arms forward.

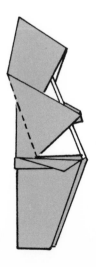

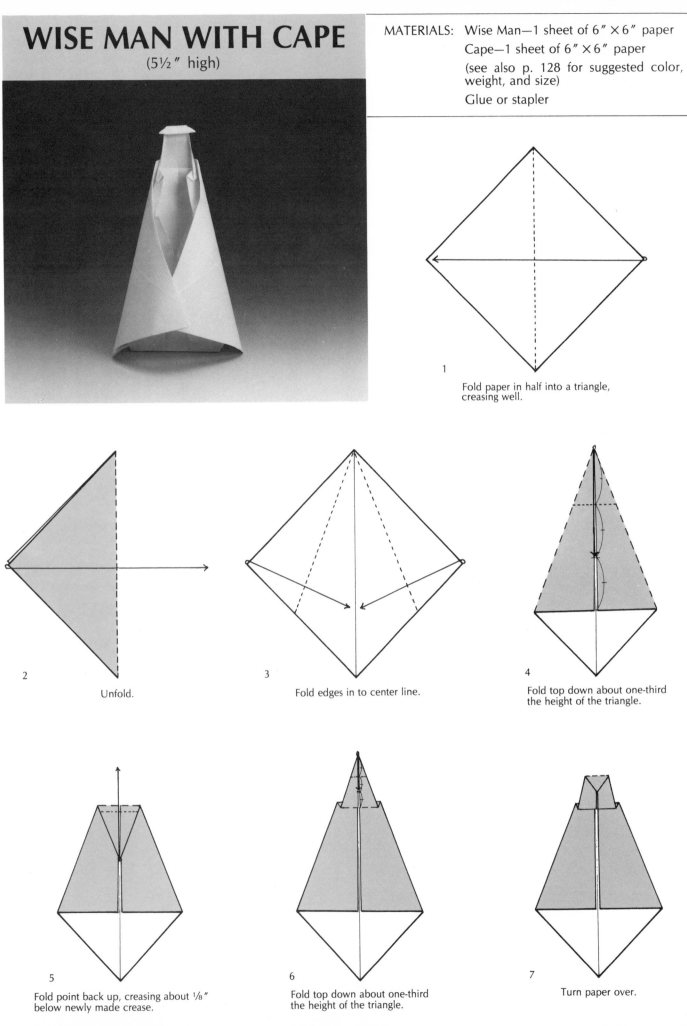

WISE MAN WITH CAPE
(5½″ high)

MATERIALS: Wise Man—1 sheet of 6″ × 6″ paper
Cape—1 sheet of 6″ × 6″ paper
(see also p. 128 for suggested color, weight, and size)
Glue or stapler

1 Fold paper in half into a triangle, creasing well.

2 Unfold.

3 Fold edges in to center line.

4 Fold top down about one-third the height of the triangle.

5 Fold point back up, creasing about ⅛″ below newly made crease.

6 Fold top down about one-third the height of the triangle.

7 Turn paper over.

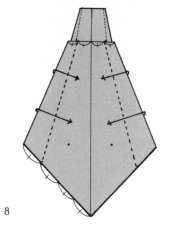

8

Fold edges in one-quarter of the way.

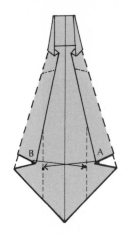

9

Pull point A over so it almost touches flap, creasing near top to take care of excess paper. Note that the head remains as it was. Bring point B over point A, creasing near top.

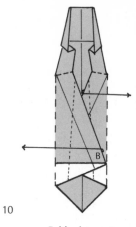

10

Fold edges out.

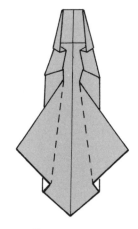

11

Turn paper over.

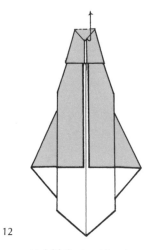

12

Unfold the top triangle, which will be the turban.

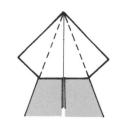

13

Cut on crease from center to edges, and open edges.

14

Turn paper over.

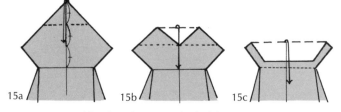

15a   15b   15c

Fold turban down one-third of the way, fold down again to top of head, then fold down again over brow.

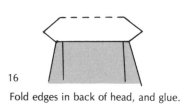

16

Fold edges in back of head, and glue.

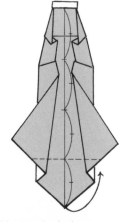

17

Fold bottom back about one-quarter of the way.

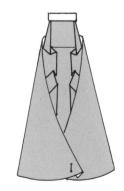

18

Make cape, put it on the Wise Man, and staple or glue it.

CAPE:

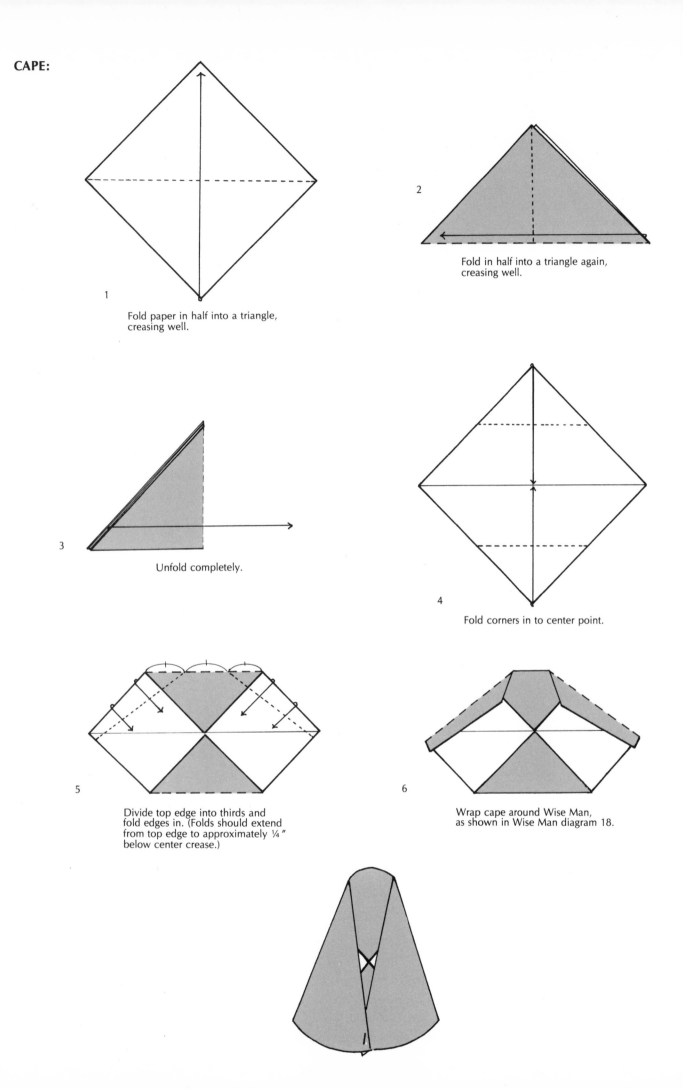

1 Fold paper in half into a triangle, creasing well.

2 Fold in half into a triangle again, creasing well.

3 Unfold completely.

4 Fold corners in to center point.

5 Divide top edge into thirds and fold edges in. (Folds should extend from top edge to approximately ¼″ below center crease.)

6 Wrap cape around Wise Man, as shown in Wise Man diagram 18.

ANGEL (5″ high)

MATERIALS: 1 sheet of 6″ × 6″ paper

(see also p. 124 and p. 126 for suggested color, weight, and size)

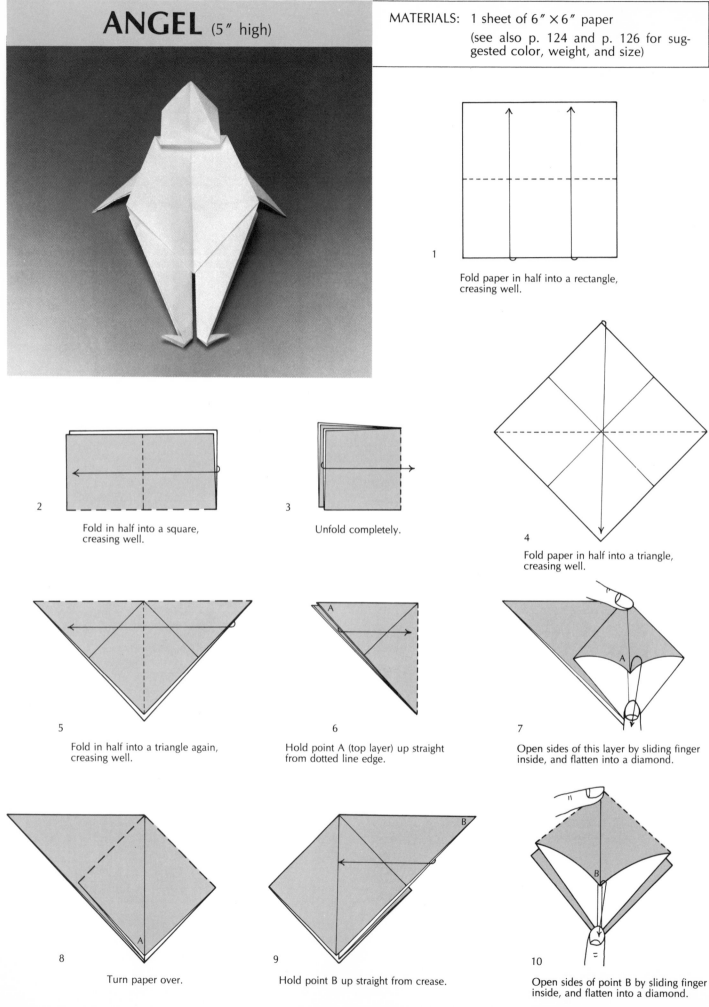

1

Fold paper in half into a rectangle, creasing well.

2

Fold in half into a square, creasing well.

3

Unfold completely.

4

Fold paper in half into a triangle, creasing well.

5

Fold in half into a triangle again, creasing well.

6

Hold point A (top layer) up straight from dotted line edge.

7

Open sides of this layer by sliding finger inside, and flatten into a diamond.

8

Turn paper over.

9

Hold point B up straight from crease.

10

Open sides of point B by sliding finger inside, and flatten into a diamond.

78

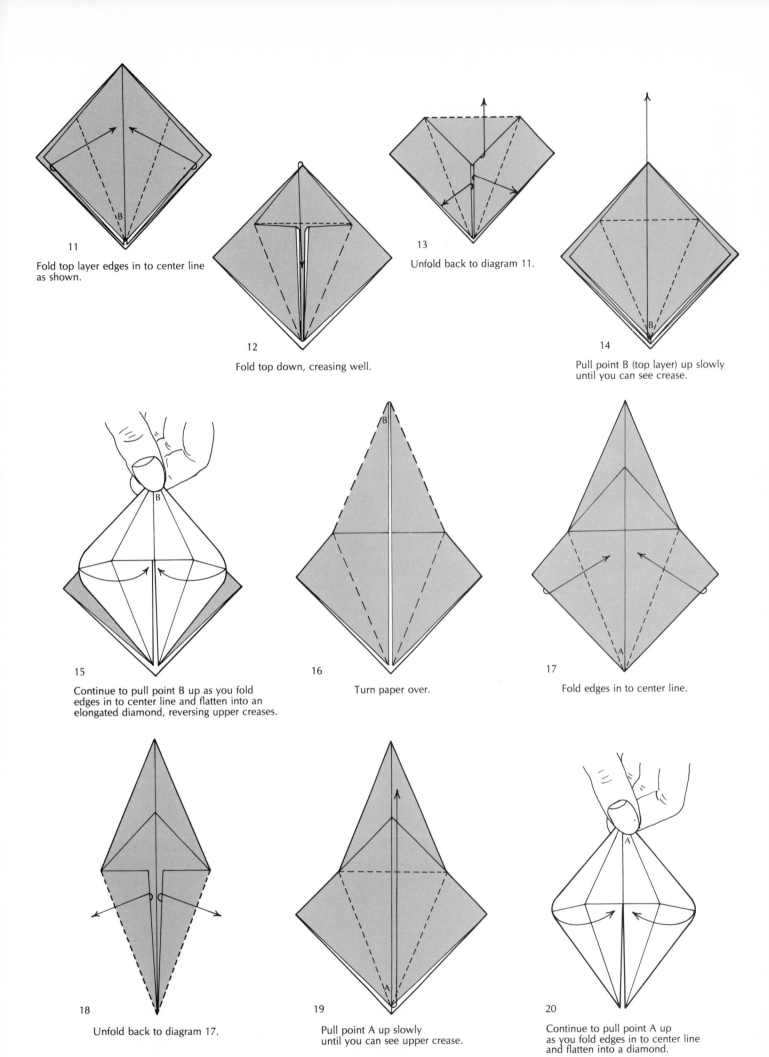

11

Fold top layer edges in to center line as shown.

12

Fold top down, creasing well.

13

Unfold back to diagram 11.

14

Pull point B (top layer) up slowly until you can see crease.

15

Continue to pull point B up as you fold edges in to center line and flatten into an elongated diamond, reversing upper creases.

16

Turn paper over.

17

Fold edges in to center line.

18

Unfold back to diagram 17.

19

Pull point A up slowly until you can see upper crease.

20

Continue to pull point A up as you fold edges in to center line and flatten into a diamond.

79

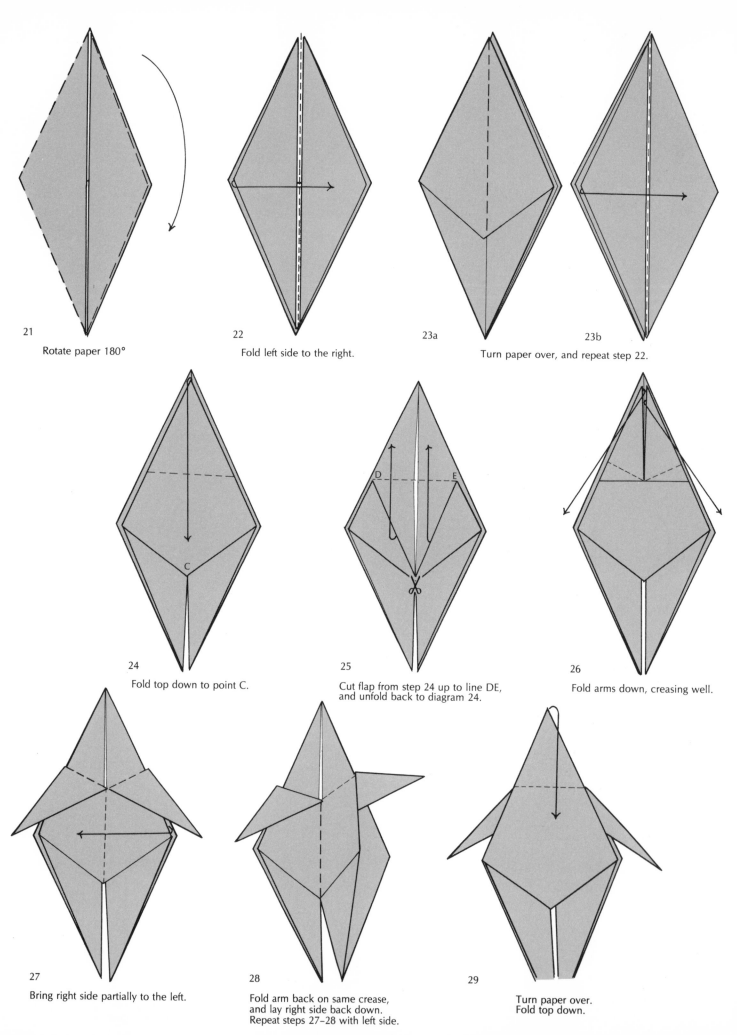

21
Rotate paper 180°

22
Fold left side to the right.

23a

23b
Turn paper over, and repeat step 22.

24
Fold top down to point C.

25
Cut flap from step 24 up to line DE,
and unfold back to diagram 24.

26
Fold arms down, creasing well.

27
Bring right side partially to the left.

28
Fold arm back on same crease,
and lay right side back down.
Repeat steps 27–28 with left side.

29
Turn paper over.
Fold top down.

80

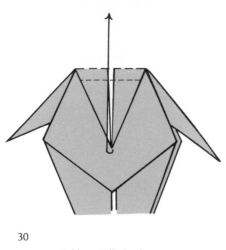

30

Fold partially back up.

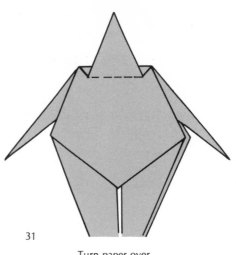

31

Turn paper over.

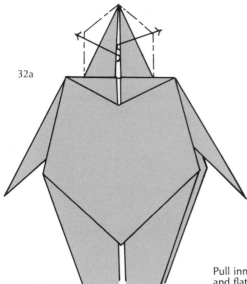

32a

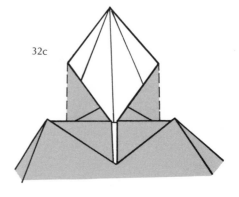

32b

32c

Pull inner edges of face out a little,
and flatten to make face rounder.

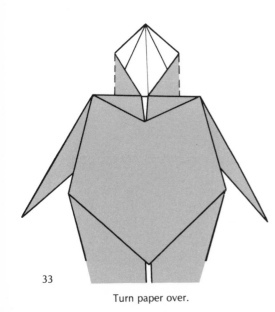

33

Turn paper over.

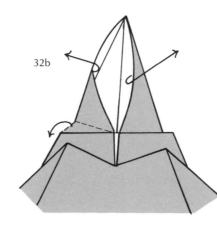

34a   34b

34c   34d

Fold feet, pull edges apart,
and reverse creases as shown.

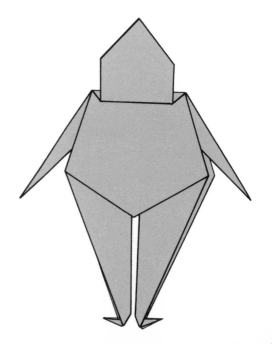

REINDEER A (5" high)

MATERIALS: 1 sheet of 6" × 6" paper
(see also p. 142 for suggested color, weight, and size)
Glue

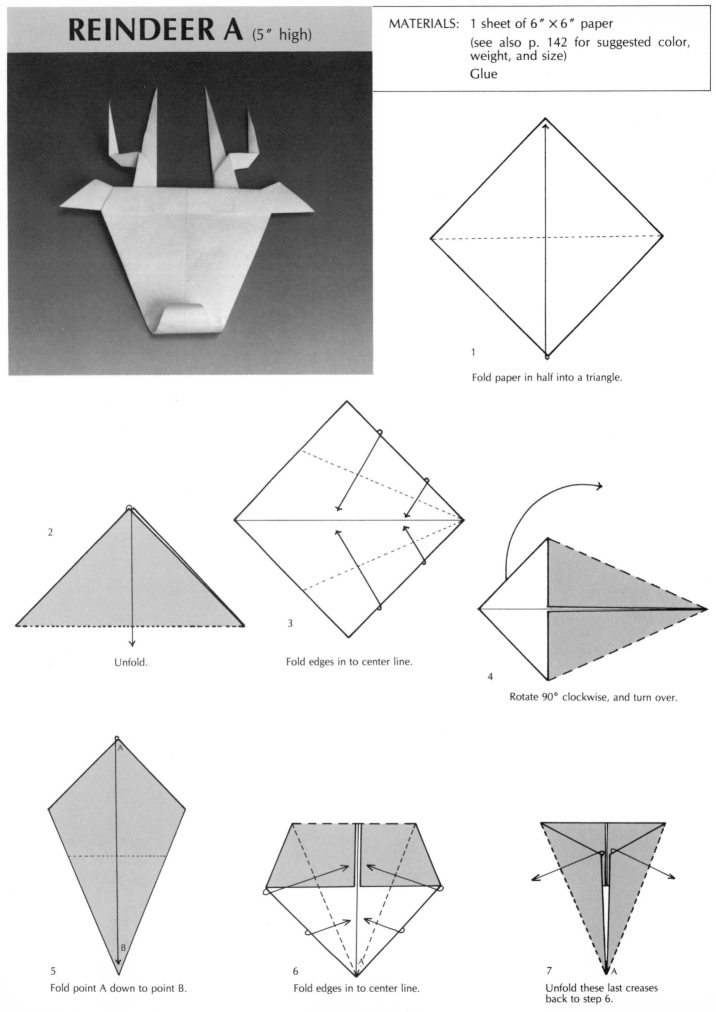

1 Fold paper in half into a triangle.

2 Unfold.

3 Fold edges in to center line.

4 Rotate 90° clockwise, and turn over.

5 Fold point A down to point B.

6 Fold edges in to center line.

7 Unfold these last creases back to step 6.

82

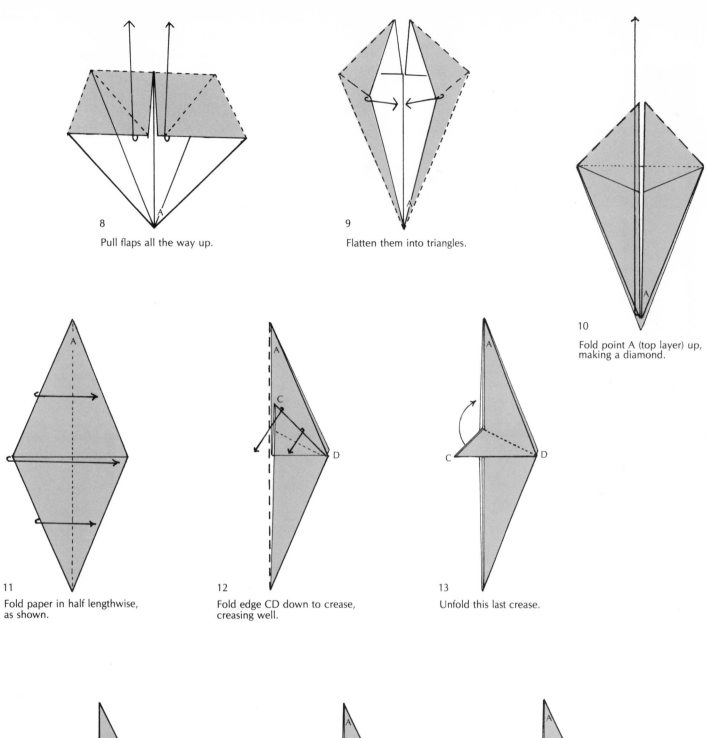

8
Pull flaps all the way up.

9
Flatten them into triangles.

10
Fold point A (top layer) up, making a diamond.

11
Fold paper in half lengthwise, as shown.

12
Fold edge CD down to crease, creasing well.

13
Unfold this last crease.

14
Hold point C straight up from crease.

15
Open sides by sliding finger inside, and flatten into a kite, creasing well.

16
Turn paper over, and repeat steps 12-15. Turn paper over again.

83

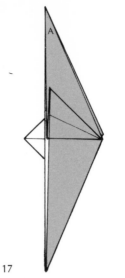

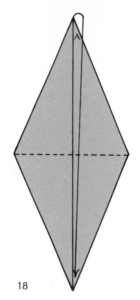

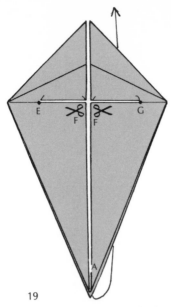

17

Unfold back to diagram 12
by unfolding kite
to make a small triangle;
turn paper over and repeat.

18

Unfold center crease and flatten
to make large diamond. Fold top
point toward you and down.

19

Cut both layers of paper two-thirds
of the way from F to E and F to G;
be careful not to cut the folded layer
underneath. Then fold point B back and
up to form a diamond.

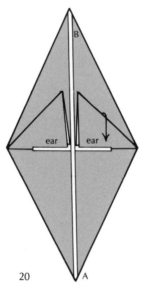

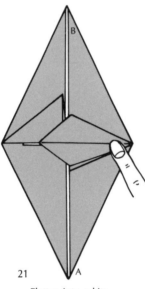

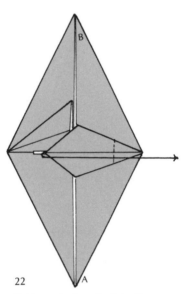

20

Hold right ear straight up
from crease.

21

Flatten into a kite.

22

Fold out the length of the line.

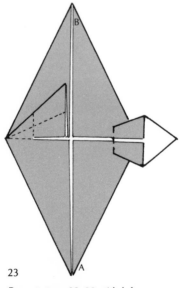

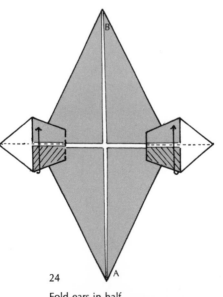

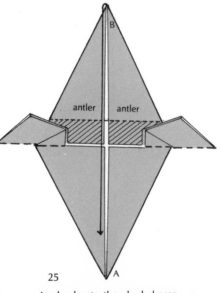

23

Repeat steps 20–22 with left ear.

24

Fold ears in half
and glue halves together.

25

Apply glue to the shaded area
and fold point B down.

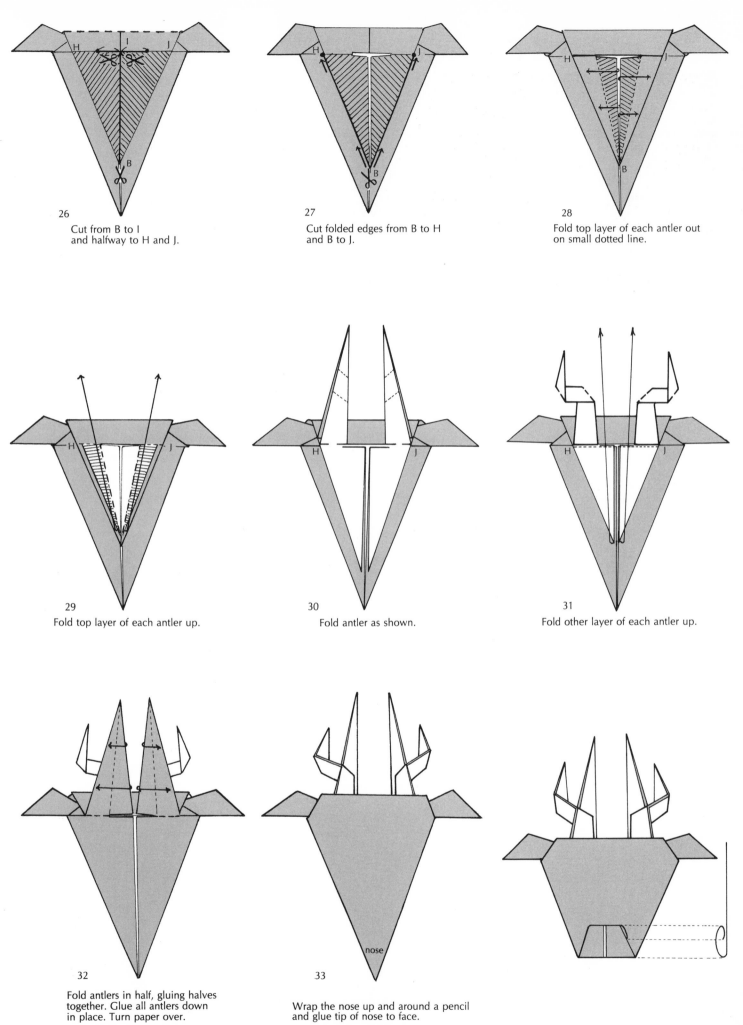

26

Cut from B to I
and halfway to H and J.

27

Cut folded edges from B to H
and B to J.

28

Fold top layer of each antler out
on small dotted line.

29

Fold top layer of each antler up.

30

Fold antler as shown.

31

Fold other layer of each antler up.

32

Fold antlers in half, gluing halves
together. Glue all antlers down
in place. Turn paper over.

33

Wrap the nose up and around a pencil
and glue tip of nose to face.

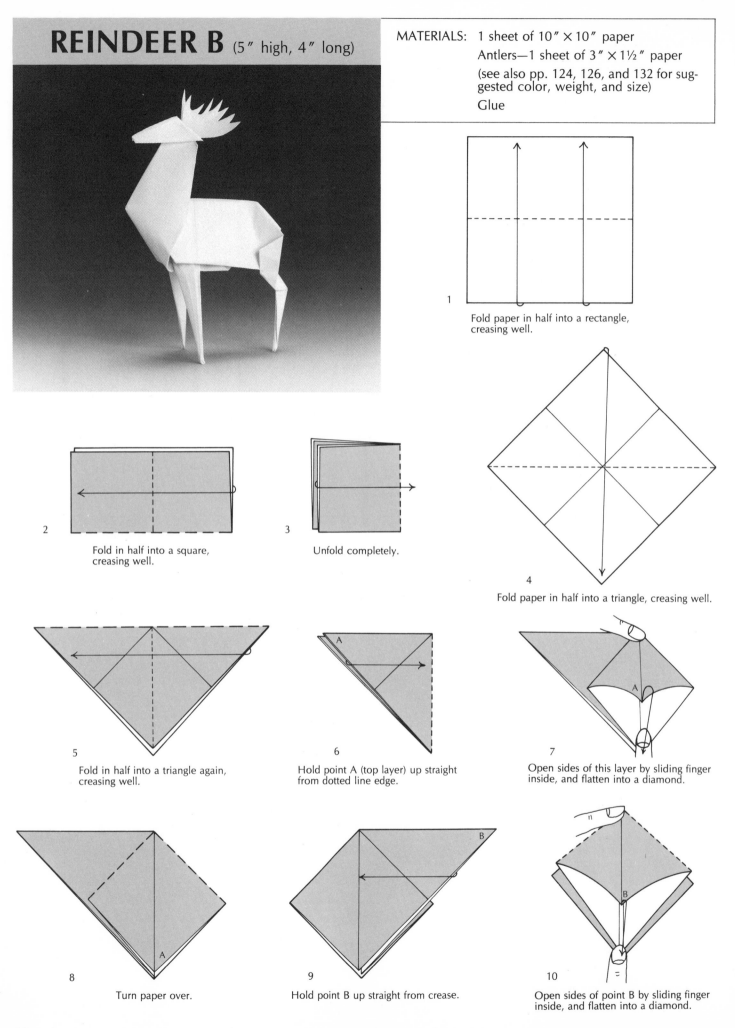

REINDEER B (5″ high, 4″ long)

MATERIALS: 1 sheet of 10″ × 10″ paper
Antlers—1 sheet of 3″ × 1½″ paper
(see also pp. 124, 126, and 132 for suggested color, weight, and size)
Glue

1

Fold paper in half into a rectangle, creasing well.

2

Fold in half into a square, creasing well.

3

Unfold completely.

4

Fold paper in half into a triangle, creasing well.

5

Fold in half into a triangle again, creasing well.

6

Hold point A (top layer) up straight from dotted line edge.

7

Open sides of this layer by sliding finger inside, and flatten into a diamond.

8

Turn paper over.

9

Hold point B up straight from crease.

10

Open sides of point B by sliding finger inside, and flatten into a diamond.

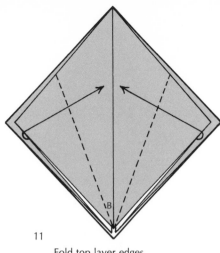

11

Fold top layer edges
in to center line as shown.

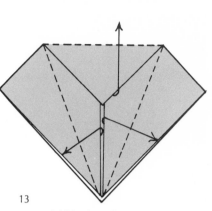

12

Fold top down, creasing well.

13

Unfold back to diagram 11.

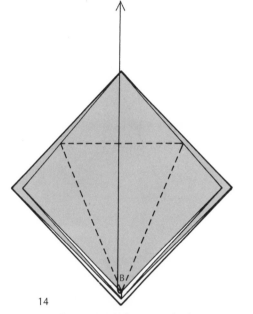

14

Pull point B (top layer) up slowly
until you can see crease.

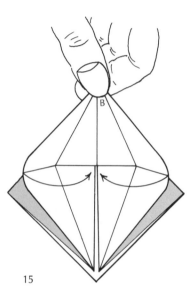

15

Continue to pull point B up as you fold
edges in to center line and flatten into an
elongated diamond, reversing upper creases.

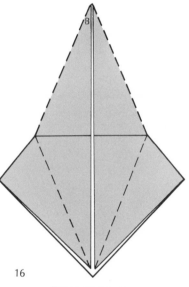

16

Turn paper over.

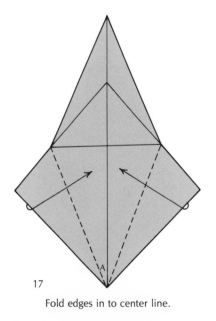

17

Fold edges in to center line.

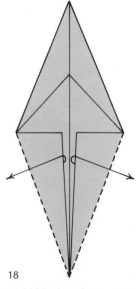

18

Unfold back to diagram 17.

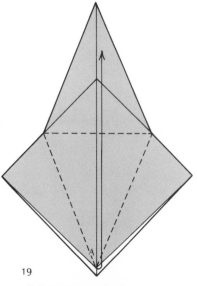

19

Pull point A up slowly
until you can see upper crease.

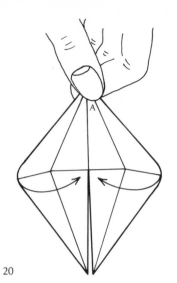

20

Continue to pull point A up
as you fold edges in to center line
and flatten into a diamond.

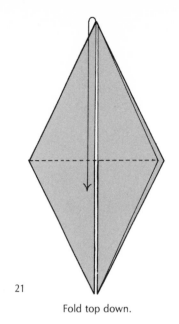

21

Fold top down.

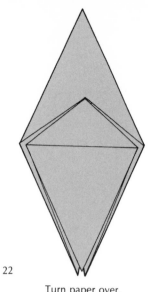

22

Turn paper over.

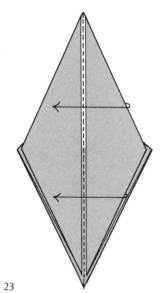

23

Fold right side (top layer) to the left.

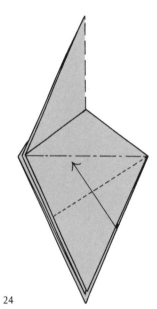

24

Fold right edge (top layer) up to the crease,
creasing well.

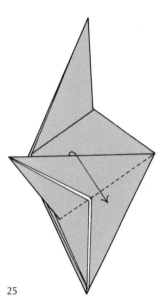

25

Unfold back to diagram 24.

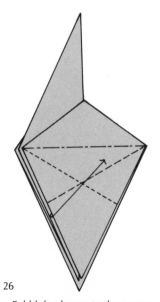

26

Fold left edge up to the crease,
creasing well.

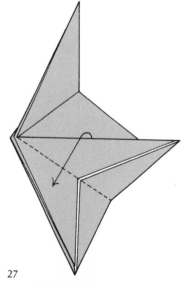

27

Unfold back to diagram 26.

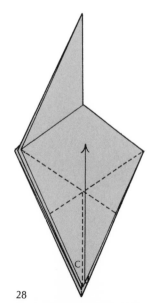

28

Hold point C (top layer) straight up
from intersection of dotted lines.

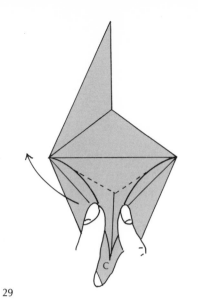

29

Pinch sides together with thumb and index finger;
press down so point stands straight up.
Fold point C to the left.

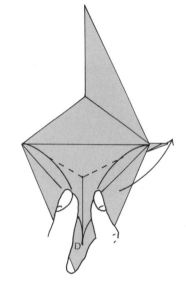

30

Fold edge up to broken dotted line,
as shown.

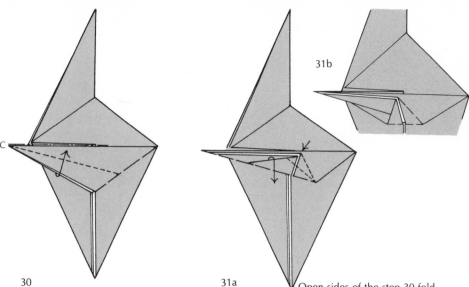
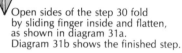

31a

31b

Open sides of the step 30 fold
by sliding finger inside and flatten,
as shown in diagram 31a.
Diagram 31b shows the finished step.

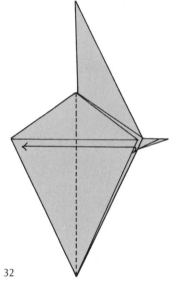

32

Turn paper over. Repeat steps 23–28.

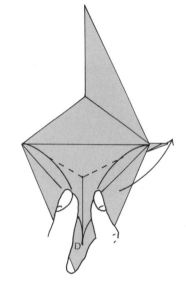

33

Then fold point D to the right.

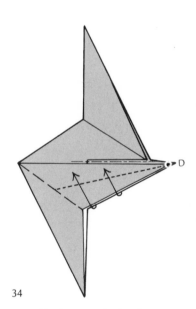

34

Fold edge up to broken line,
as shown.

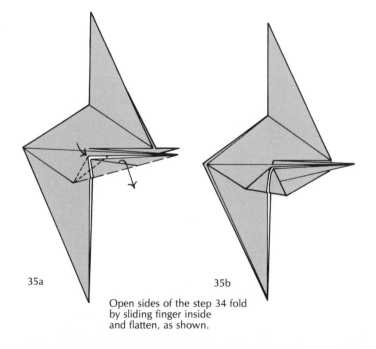

35a

35b

Open sides of the step 34 fold
by sliding finger inside
and flatten, as shown.

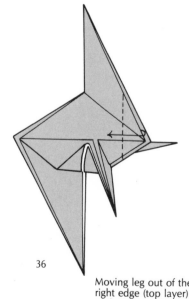

36

Moving leg out of the way, fold
right edge (top layer) to the left one-third
of the way to the center fold, creasing well.

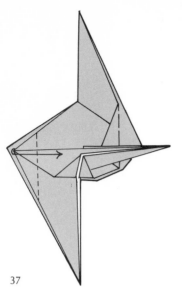

37

Fold left side (top layer) to the right one-third of the way, creasing well.

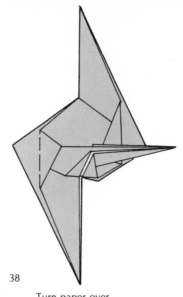

38

Turn paper over, and repeat steps 36–37.

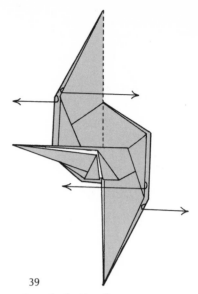

39

Open both sides, flatten, and turn so right side is facing you.

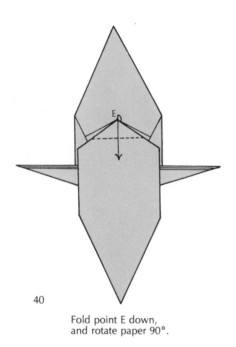

40

Fold point E down, and rotate paper 90°.

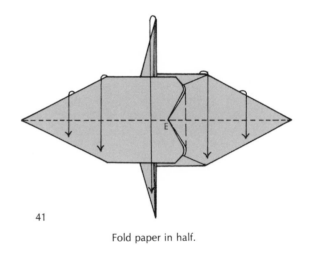

41

Fold paper in half.

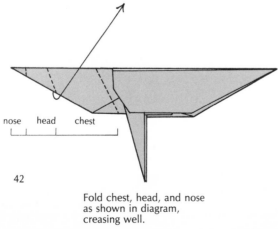

nose   head   chest

42

Fold chest, head, and nose as shown in diagram, creasing well.

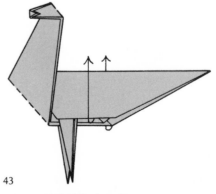

43

Unfold back to diagram 41.

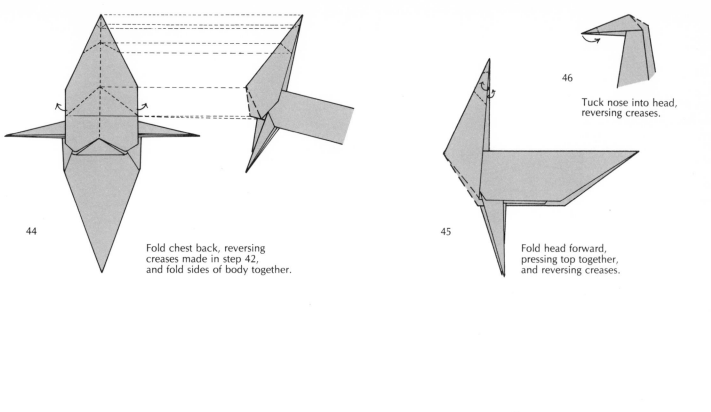

44

Fold chest back, reversing
creases made in step 42,
and fold sides of body together.

45

Fold head forward,
pressing top together,
and reversing creases.

46

Tuck nose into head,
reversing creases.

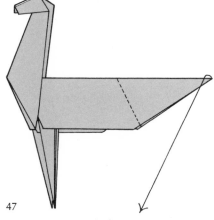

47

Fold right side down
making hind leg a little longer
than front ones. Crease well.

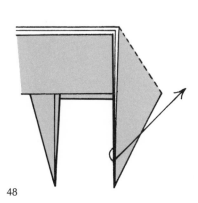

48

Unfold back to diagram 47.

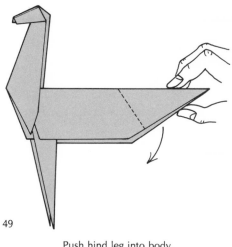

49

Push hind leg into body,
reversing creases.

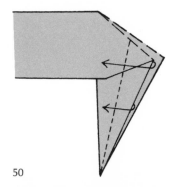

50

Fold top layer of hind leg in half.

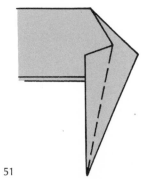

51

Turn paper over, and repeat step 50.

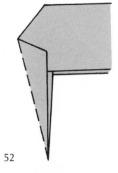

52

Turn paper over.

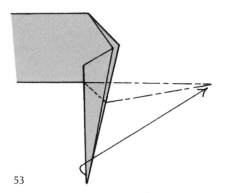

53

Fold leg on small dotted line up to broken line.

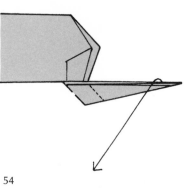

54

Fold end down on small dotted line.

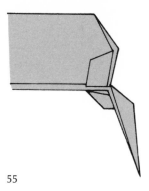

55

Unfold back to diagram 49.

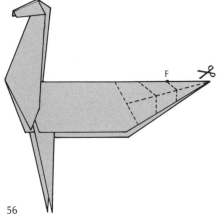

56

Cut top on crease to point F, and fold back to diagram 52.

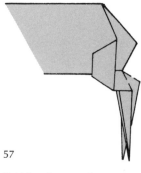

57

Fold legs by reversing creases made in step 53, and fold end down, reversing creases made in step 54.

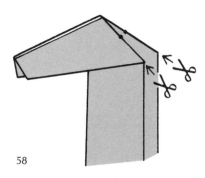

58

Cut halfway in on head creases.

59

Push head down a little so ears stick out.

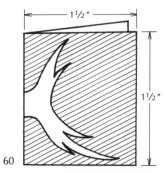

60

1½"

1½"

Fold paper in half.
Draw antler, and cut away shaded part.

61

Open head, and glue ends of antlers inside.

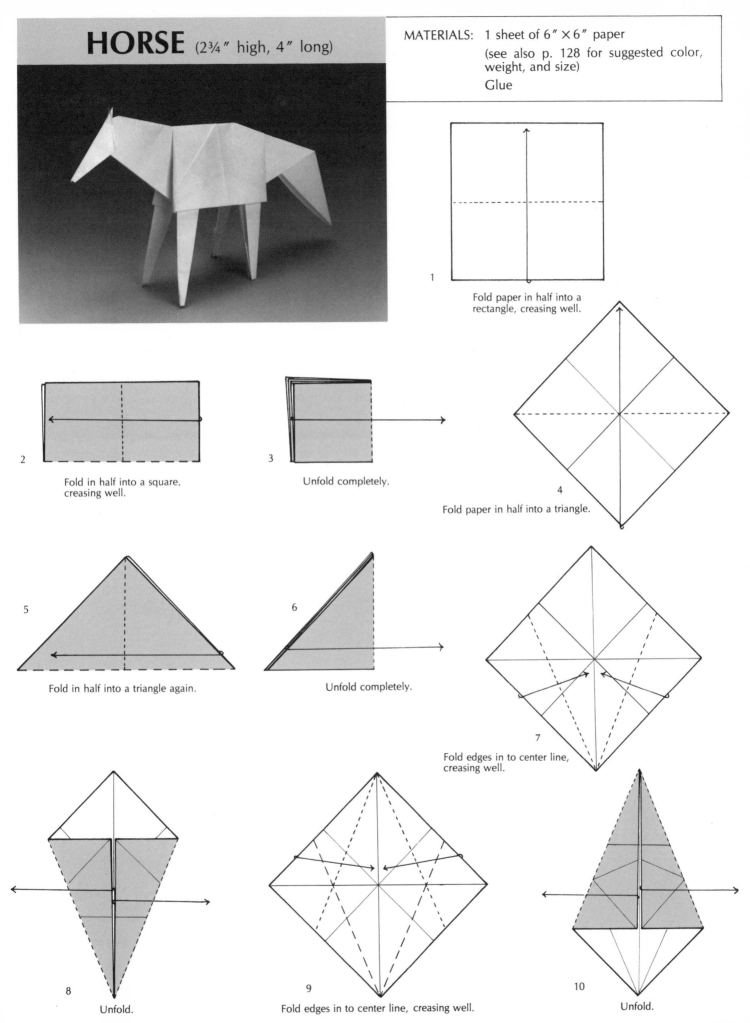

HORSE (2¾″ high, 4″ long)

MATERIALS: 1 sheet of 6″ × 6″ paper
(see also p. 128 for suggested color, weight, and size)
Glue

1 Fold paper in half into a rectangle, creasing well.

2 Fold in half into a square, creasing well.

3 Unfold completely.

4 Fold paper in half into a triangle.

5 Fold in half into a triangle again.

6 Unfold completely.

7 Fold edges in to center line, creasing well.

8 Unfold.

9 Fold edges in to center line, creasing well.

10 Unfold.

93

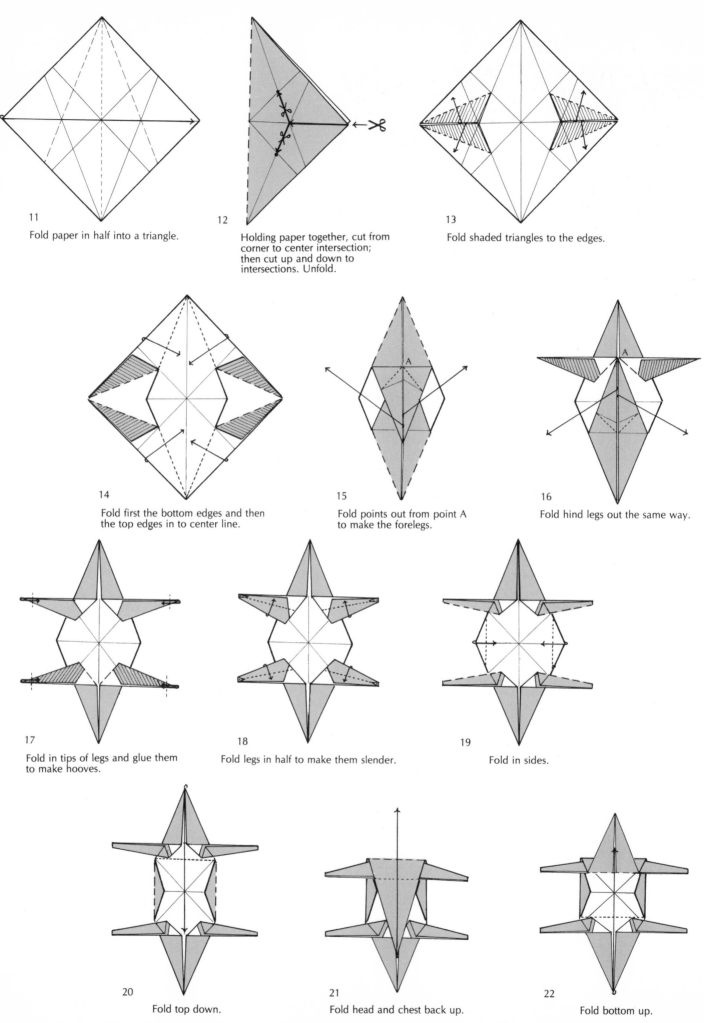

11

Fold paper in half into a triangle.

12

Holding paper together, cut from corner to center intersection; then cut up and down to intersections. Unfold.

13

Fold shaded triangles to the edges.

14

Fold first the bottom edges and then the top edges in to center line.

15

Fold points out from point A to make the forelegs.

16

Fold hind legs out the same way.

17

Fold in tips of legs and glue them to make hooves.

18

Fold legs in half to make them slender.

19

Fold in sides.

20

Fold top down.

21

Fold head and chest back up.

22

Fold bottom up.

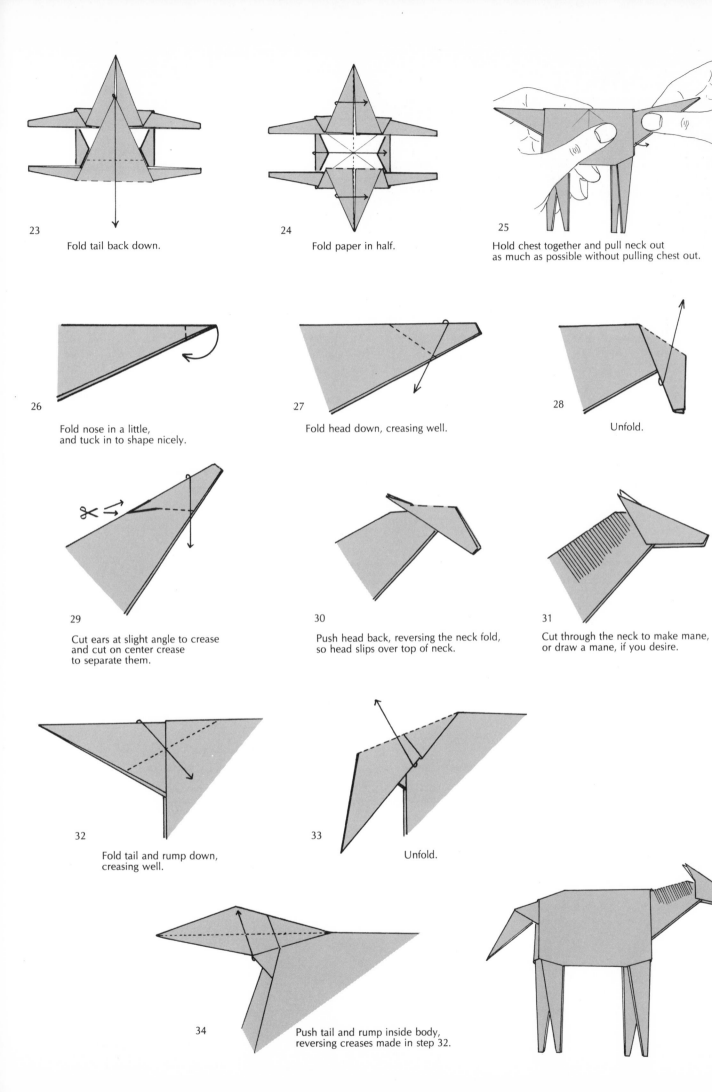

23
Fold tail back down.

24
Fold paper in half.

25
Hold chest together and pull neck out
as much as possible without pulling chest out.

26
Fold nose in a little,
and tuck in to shape nicely.

27
Fold head down, creasing well.

28
Unfold.

29
Cut ears at slight angle to crease
and cut on center crease
to separate them.

30
Push head back, reversing the neck fold,
so head slips over top of neck.

31
Cut through the neck to make mane,
or draw a mane, if you desire.

32
Fold tail and rump down,
creasing well.

33
Unfold.

34
Push tail and rump inside body,
reversing creases made in step 32.

CAMEL (4″ high, 4½″ long)

MATERIALS: 1 sheet of 10″ × 10″ paper

(see also p. 128 for suggested color, weight, and size)

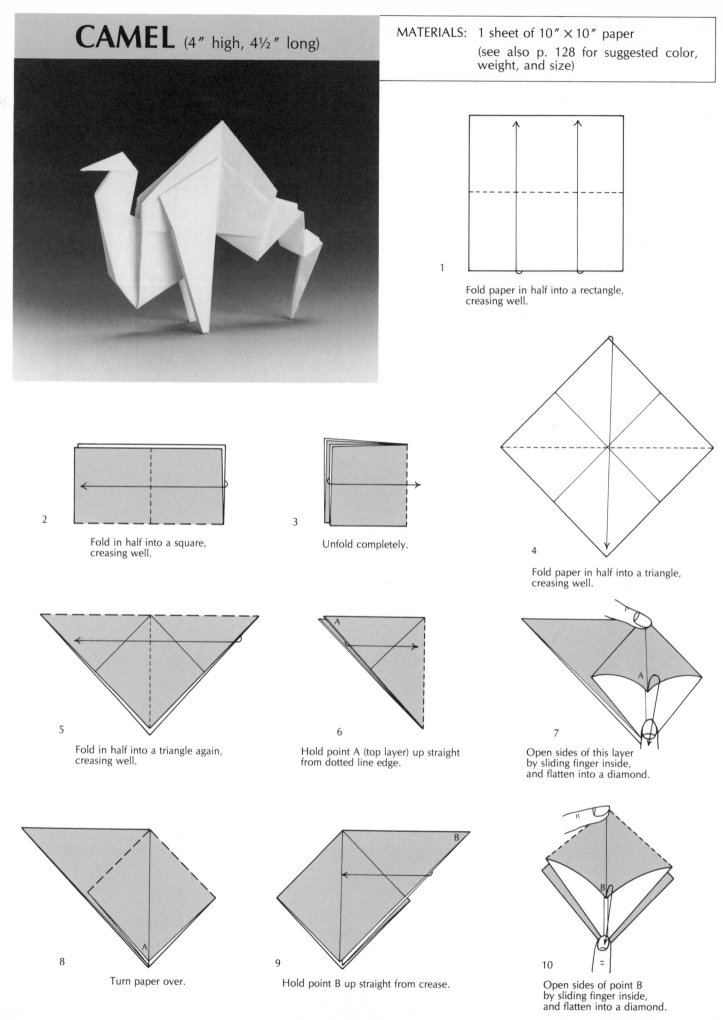

1 Fold paper in half into a rectangle, creasing well.

2 Fold in half into a square, creasing well.

3 Unfold completely.

4 Fold paper in half into a triangle, creasing well.

5 Fold in half into a triangle again, creasing well.

6 Hold point A (top layer) up straight from dotted line edge.

7 Open sides of this layer by sliding finger inside, and flatten into a diamond.

8 Turn paper over.

9 Hold point B up straight from crease.

10 Open sides of point B by sliding finger inside, and flatten into a diamond.

96

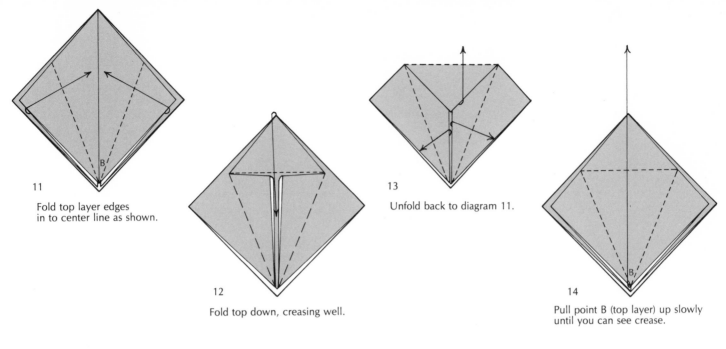

11
Fold top layer edges
in to center line as shown.

12
Fold top down, creasing well.

13
Unfold back to diagram 11.

14
Pull point B (top layer) up slowly
until you can see crease.

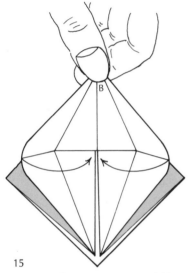

15
Continue to pull point B up as you fold
edges in to center line and flatten into
an elongated diamond, reversing upper creases.

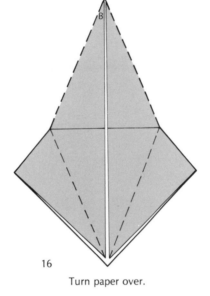

16
Turn paper over.

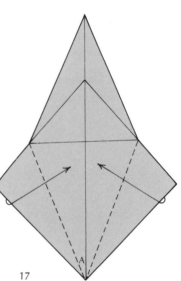

17
· Fold edges in to center line.

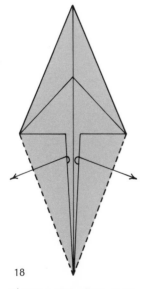

18
Unfold back to diagram 17.

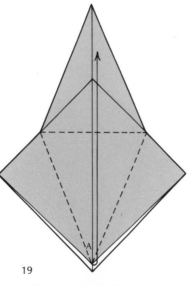

19
Pull point A up slowly
until you can see upper crease.

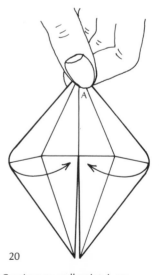

20
Continue to pull point A up
as you fold edges in to center line
and flatten into a diamond.

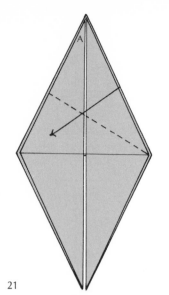

21

Fold top right edge (top layer) down to center line, creasing well.

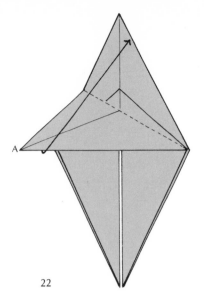

22

Unfold back to diagram 21.

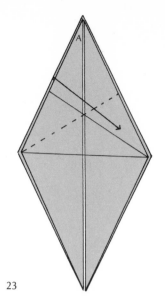

23

Fold top left edge (top layer) down to center line, creasing well.

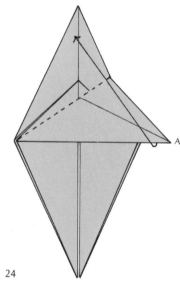

24

Unfold back to diagram 23.

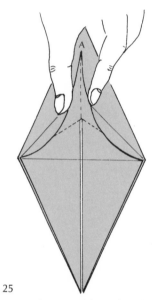

25

Hold point A (top layer) straight up from intersection of dotted lines, pinching sides together with thumb and index finger; press down so point stands straight up from intersection of fold lines.

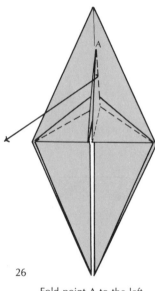

26

Fold point A to the left, creasing well.

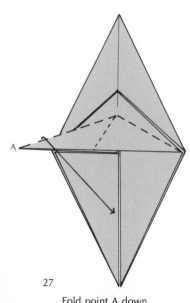

27

Fold point A down on small dotted line so edge lies on center line.

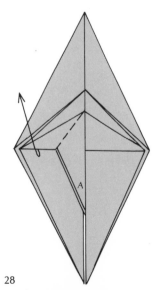

28

Following the arrow, lift up bottom left edge of triangle and flatten, creasing well.

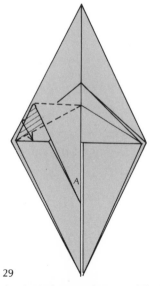

29

Push edge in between layers and flatten.

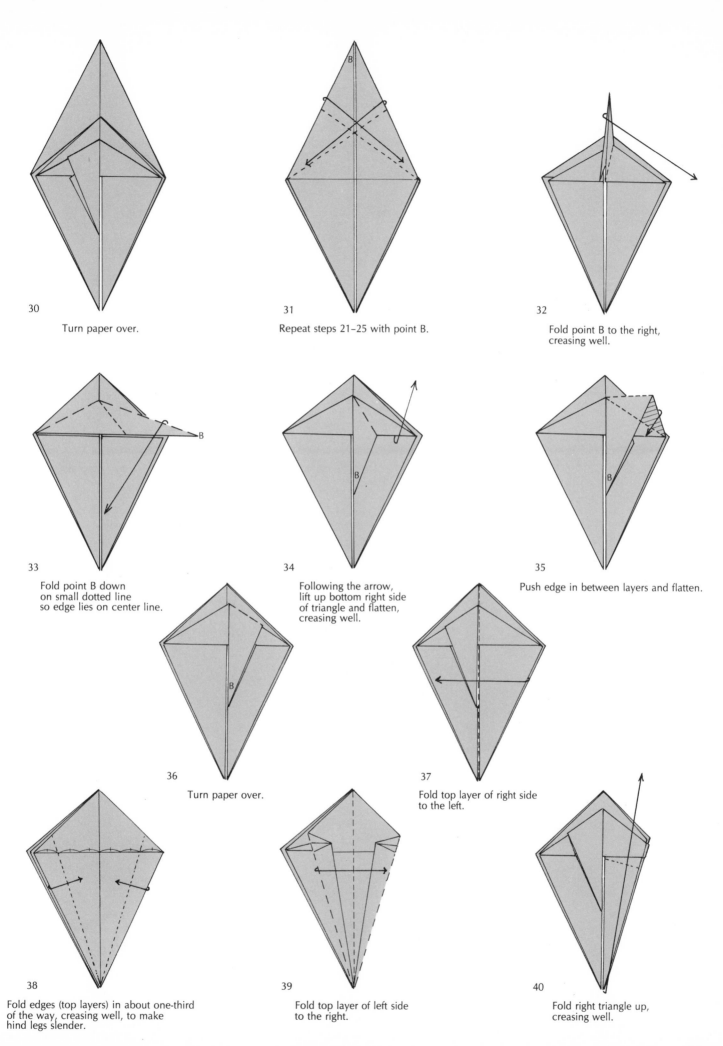

30

Turn paper over.

31

Repeat steps 21–25 with point B.

32

Fold point B to the right, creasing well.

33

Fold point B down on small dotted line so edge lies on center line.

34

Following the arrow, lift up bottom right side of triangle and flatten, creasing well.

35

Push edge in between layers and flatten.

36

Turn paper over.

37

Fold top layer of right side to the left.

38

Fold edges (top layers) in about one-third of the way, creasing well, to make hind legs slender.

39

Fold top layer of left side to the right.

40

Fold right triangle up, creasing well.

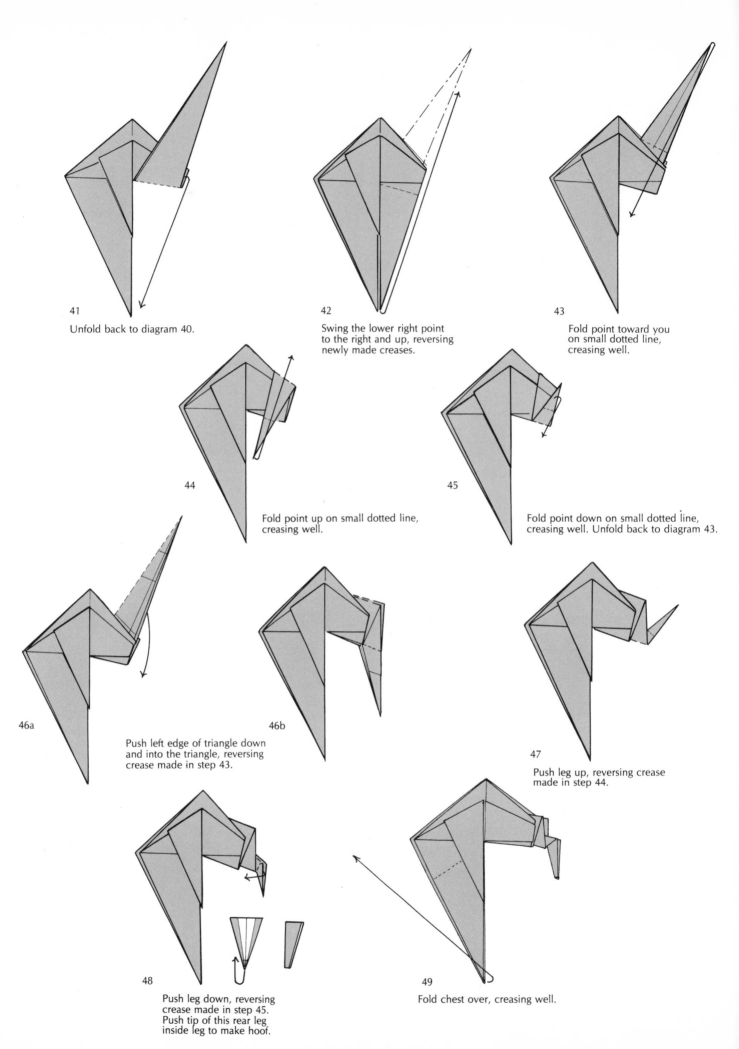

41
Unfold back to diagram 40.

42
Swing the lower right point to the right and up, reversing newly made creases.

43
Fold point toward you on small dotted line, creasing well.

44
Fold point up on small dotted line, creasing well.

45
Fold point down on small dotted line, creasing well. Unfold back to diagram 43.

46a

46b
Push left edge of triangle down and into the triangle, reversing crease made in step 43.

47
Push leg up, reversing crease made in step 44.

48
Push leg down, reversing crease made in step 45. Push tip of this rear leg inside leg to make hoof.

49
Fold chest over, creasing well.

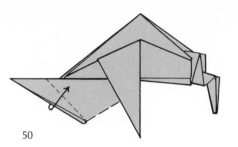

50

Fold neck up, creasing well.

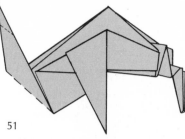

51

Fold head toward you, creasing well.

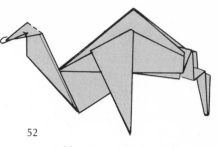

52

Fold nose up, creasing well.

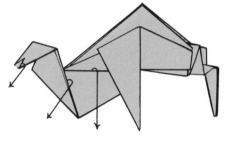

53

Unfold back to diagram 49.

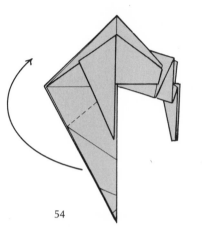

54

Push chest into body, reversing crease made in step 49.

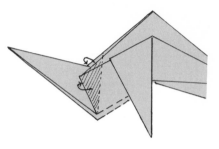

55

Tuck shaded triangles (both sides) into body, creasing well.

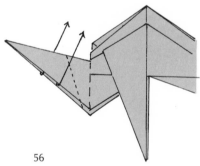

56

Push neck back over chest, reversing creases made in step 50.

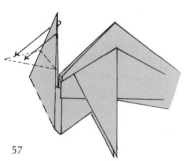

57

Fold head forward over neck, reversing creases made in step 51.

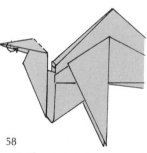

58

Tuck nose into head, reversing creases made in step 52.

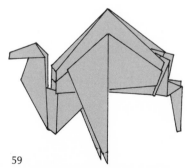

59

Fold tips of forelegs back, creasing well.

60

Unfold back to diagram 59.

61

Tuck tips of legs inside to make hooves.

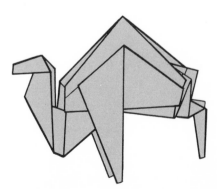

MANGER/SLEIGH
(3½" long, bottom edge)

MATERIALS: 1 sheet of 6" × 6" paper
(see also p. 128 and p. 132 for suggested color, weight, and size)

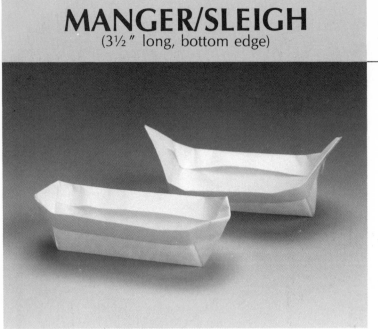

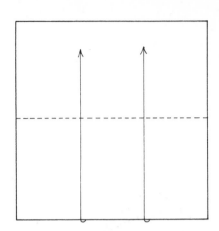

1

Fold paper in half into a rectangle, creasing well.

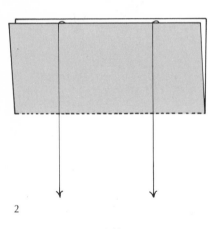

2

Unfold.

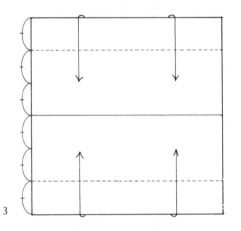

3

Fold edges in toward center one-third of the way.

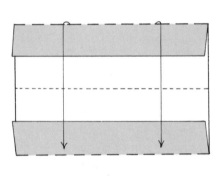

4

Fold paper in half into a rectangle.

5

Fold corners down as shown in diagram.

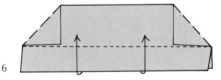

6

Fold bottom edge up.

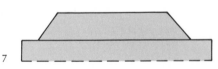

7

Turn paper over, and repeat step 6.

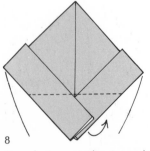

8

Open bottom, overlapping ends and folding ends inside as shown in diagram.

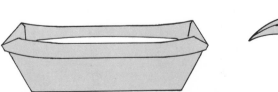

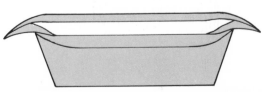

To make a sleigh, fold the ends outside.

STAR (5¾″ long)

MATERIALS: 1 sheet of 6″ × 6″ paper
(see also p. 124 for suggested color, weight, and size)

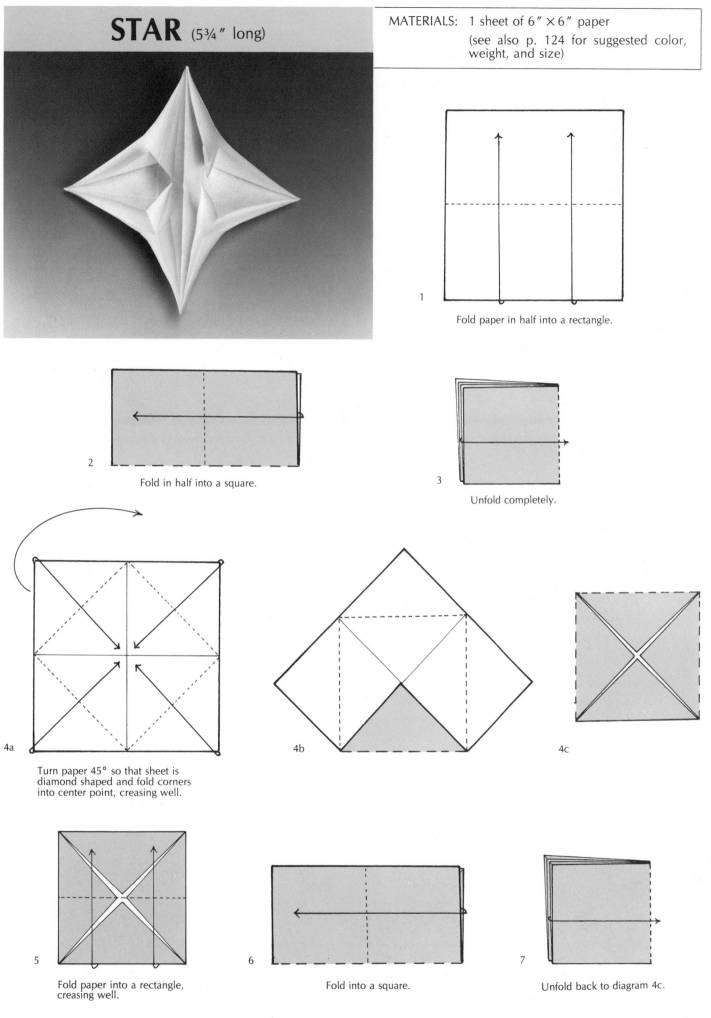

1 Fold paper in half into a rectangle.

2 Fold in half into a square.

3 Unfold completely.

4a Turn paper 45° so that sheet is diamond shaped and fold corners into center point, creasing well.

4b

4c

5 Fold paper into a rectangle, creasing well.

6 Fold into a square.

7 Unfold back to diagram 4c.

103

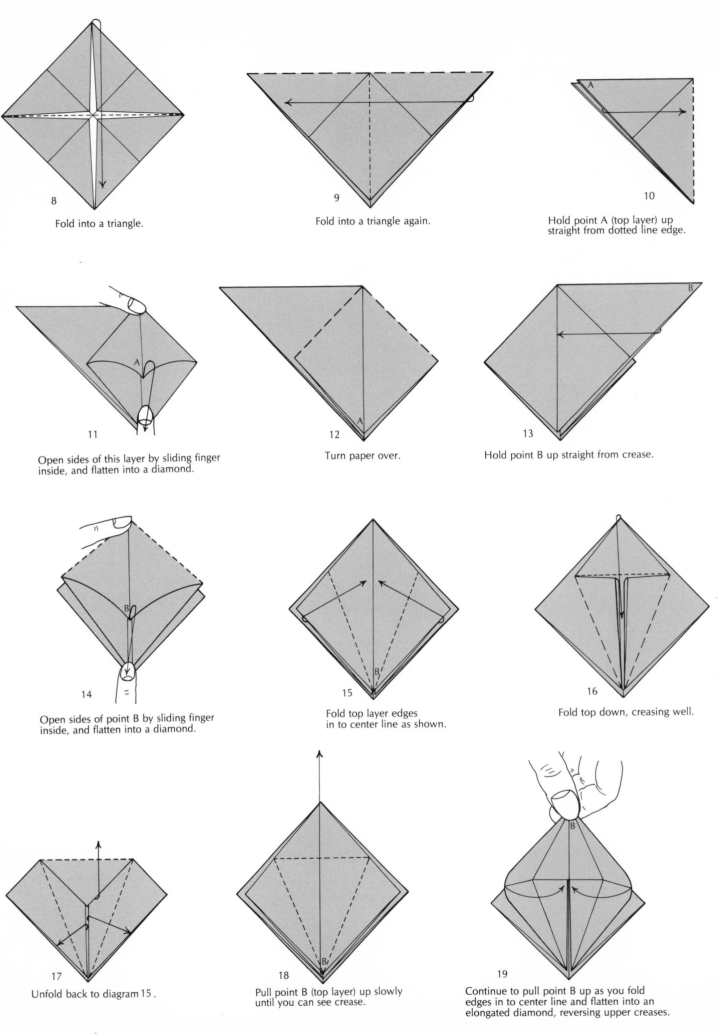

8
Fold into a triangle.

9
Fold into a triangle again.

10
Hold point A (top layer) up straight from dotted line edge.

11
Open sides of this layer by sliding finger inside, and flatten into a diamond.

12
Turn paper over.

13
Hold point B up straight from crease.

14
Open sides of point B by sliding finger inside, and flatten into a diamond.

15
Fold top layer edges in to center line as shown.

16
Fold top down, creasing well.

17
Unfold back to diagram 15.

18
Pull point B (top layer) up slowly until you can see crease.

19
Continue to pull point B up as you fold edges in to center line and flatten into an elongated diamond, reversing upper creases.

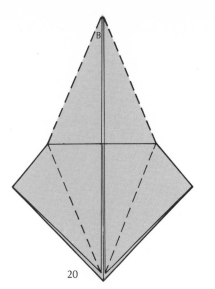

20

Turn paper over.

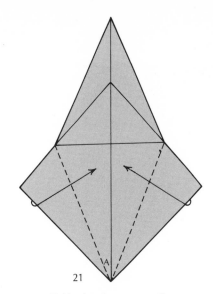

21

Fold edges in to center line.

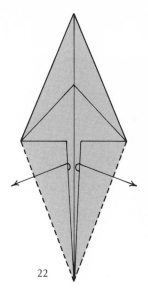

22

Unfold back to diagram 21.

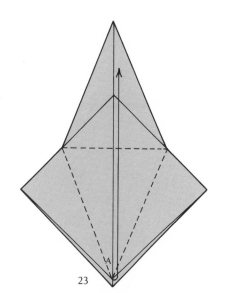

23

Pull point A up slowly
until you can see upper crease.

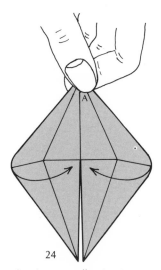

24

Continue to pull point A up
as you fold edges in to center line
and flatten into a diamond.

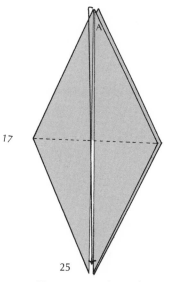

17

25

Fold point A (top layer) down.

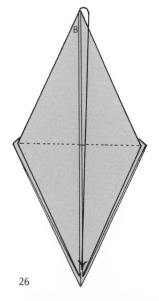

26

Turn paper over and fold point B down.

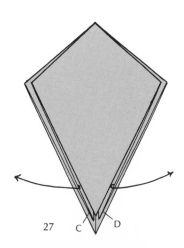

27

Pull points C and D straight out,
as shown.

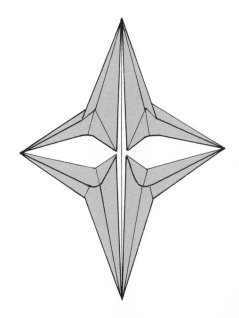

BELL (5" high)

MATERIALS: 1 sheet of 6" × 6" paper
(see also pp. 124, 126, and 137 for suggested color, weight, and size)
Glue

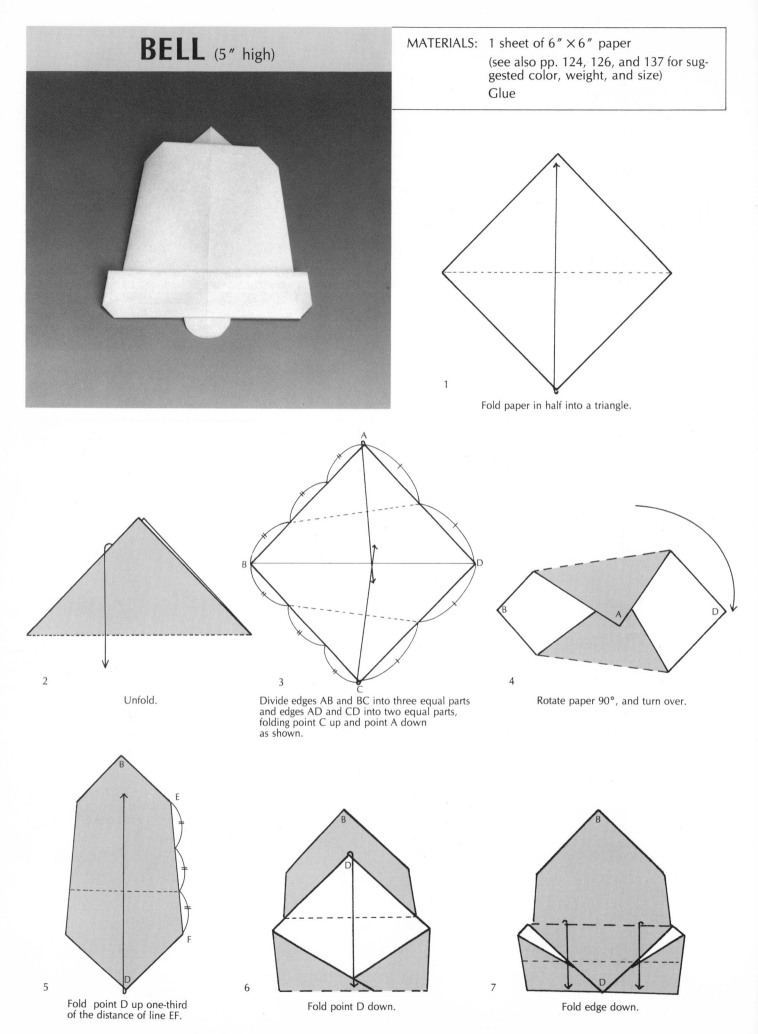

1 Fold paper in half into a triangle.

2 Unfold.

3 Divide edges AB and BC into three equal parts and edges AD and CD into two equal parts, folding point C up and point A down as shown.

4 Rotate paper 90°, and turn over.

5 Fold point D up one-third of the distance of line EF.

6 Fold point D down.

7 Fold edge down.

106

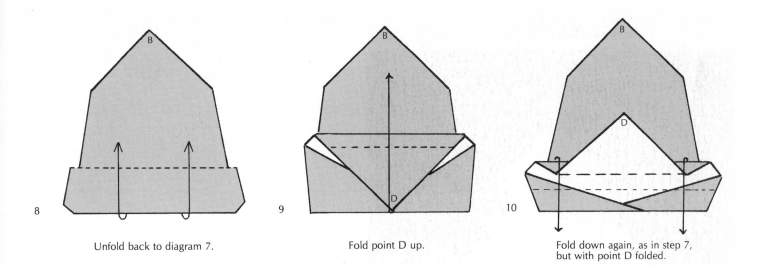

8 Unfold back to diagram 7.

9 Fold point D up.

10 Fold down again, as in step 7, but with point D folded.

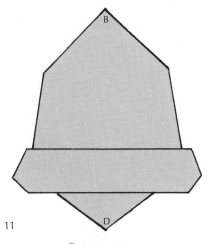

11 Turn paper over.

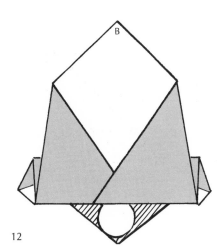

12 Draw clapper, and cut away shaded parts.

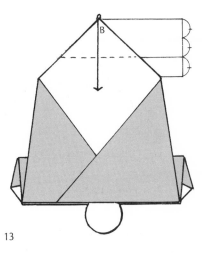

13 Fold point B down, creasing well.

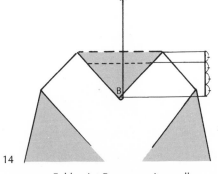

14 Fold point B up, creasing well.

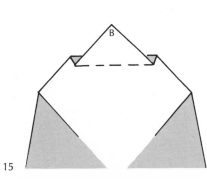

15 Turn paper over, and glue all flaps.

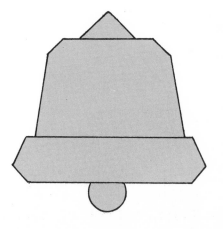

CHURCH (3½″ high)

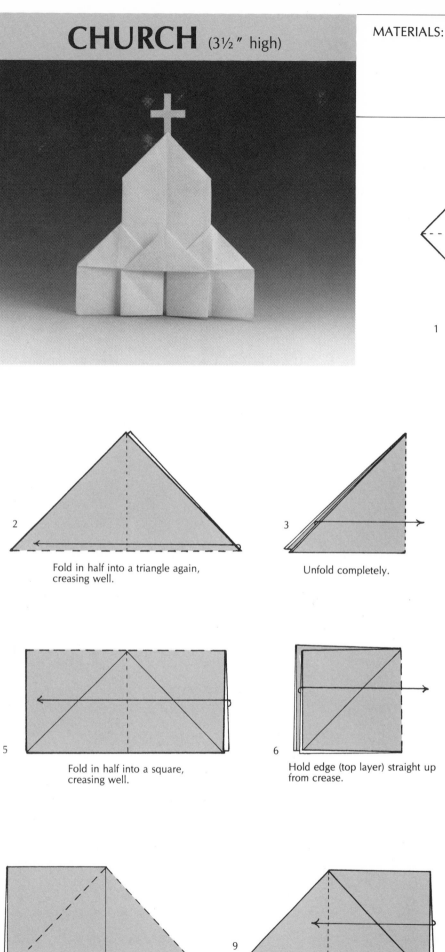

MATERIALS: 1 sheet of 6″ × 6″ paper
Cross—1 sheet of 1″ × ⅝″ paper
(see also p. 124 and p. 148 for suggested color, weight, and size)
Glue

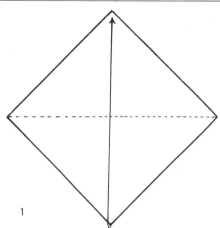

1 Fold paper in half into a triangle, creasing well.

2 Fold in half into a triangle again, creasing well.

3 Unfold completely.

4 Fold paper in half into a rectangle, creasing well.

5 Fold in half into a square, creasing well.

6 Hold edge (top layer) straight up from crease.

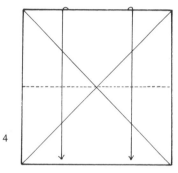

7 Open sides by sliding finger inside, and flatten into a triangle.

8 Turn paper over.

9 Hold edge straight up from crease.

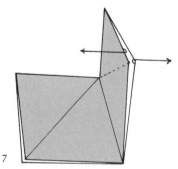

10 Open sides by sliding finger inside, and flatten into a triangle.

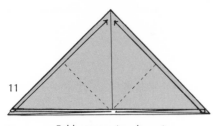

11

Fold corners (top layers)
in to center line.

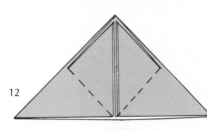

12

Turn paper over, and repeat step 11.

13

Hold sides straight up from edges.

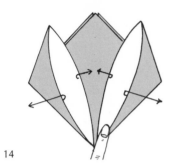

14

Open sides by sliding fingers inside,
and flatten into squares.

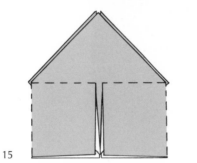

15

Turn paper over, and repeat steps 13–14.

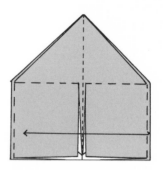

16

Fold right side (top layer) to the left.

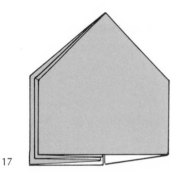

17

Turn paper over, and repeat step 16.

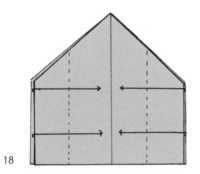

18

Fold edges (top layers) in to center line.

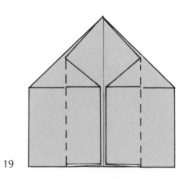

19

Turn paper over, and repeat step 18.

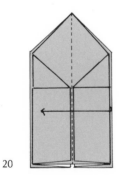

20

Fold right side to the left.

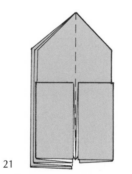

21

Turn paper over, and repeat step 20.

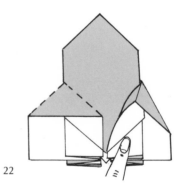

22

Open sides by sliding fingers inside,
and flatten.

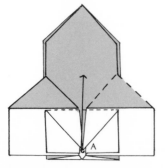

23

Fold point A up.

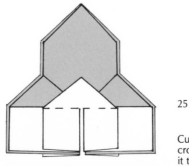

24

Turn over and repeat steps 22–23.

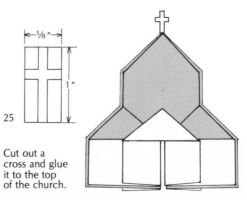

25

Cut out a
cross and glue
it to the top
of the church.

BALLOON ORNAMENT
(1½" high)

MATERIALS: 1 sheet of 6" × 6" paper
(see also p. 124 for suggested color, weight, and size)

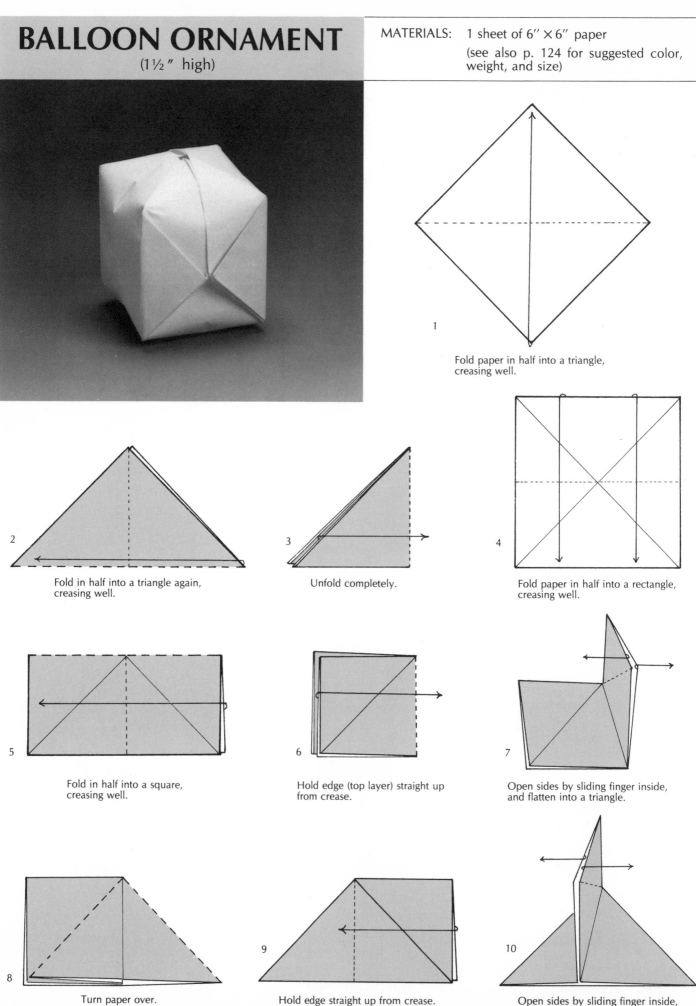

1 Fold paper in half into a triangle, creasing well.

2 Fold in half into a triangle again, creasing well.

3 Unfold completely.

4 Fold paper in half into a rectangle, creasing well.

5 Fold in half into a square, creasing well.

6 Hold edge (top layer) straight up from crease.

7 Open sides by sliding finger inside, and flatten into a triangle.

8 Turn paper over.

9 Hold edge straight up from crease.

10 Open sides by sliding finger inside, and flatten into a triangle.

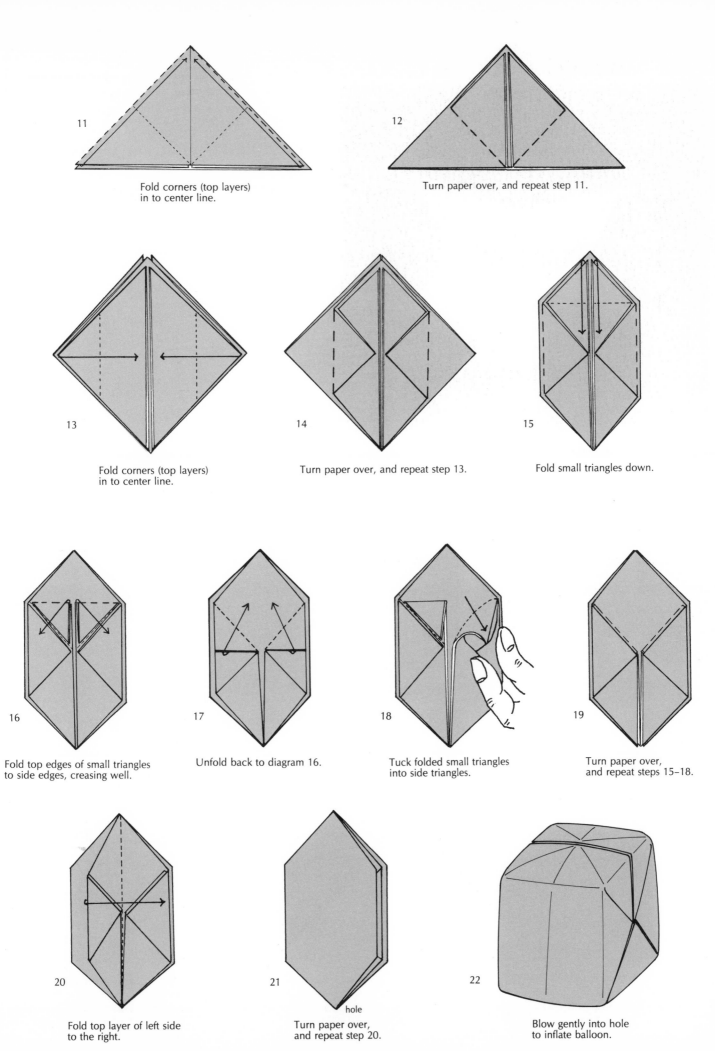

11

Fold corners (top layers)
in to center line.

12

Turn paper over, and repeat step 11.

13

Fold corners (top layers)
in to center line.

14

Turn paper over, and repeat step 13.

15

Fold small triangles down.

16

Fold top edges of small triangles
to side edges, creasing well.

17

Unfold back to diagram 16.

18

Tuck folded small triangles
into side triangles.

19

Turn paper over,
and repeat steps 15–18.

20

Fold top layer of left side
to the right.

21

hole

Turn paper over,
and repeat step 20.

22

Blow gently into hole
to inflate balloon.

BASKET A (5″ wide)

MATERIALS: 1 sheet of 6″ × 6″ paper

(see also p. 124 and p. 126 for suggested color, weight, and size)

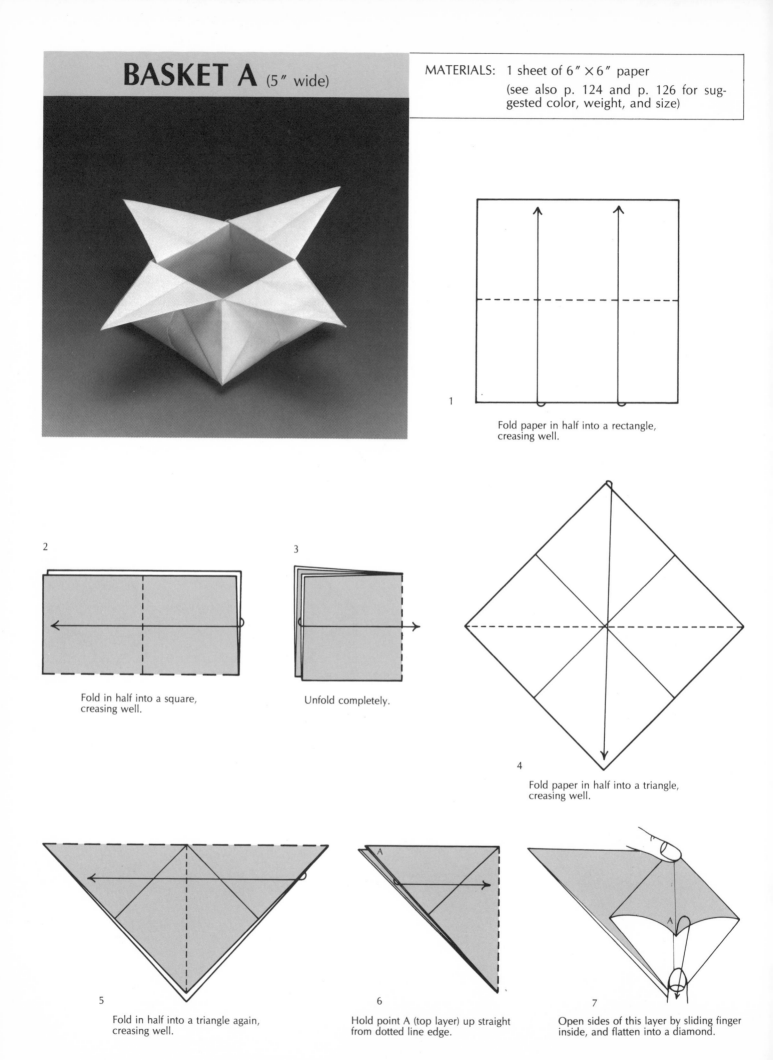

1 Fold paper in half into a rectangle, creasing well.

2 Fold in half into a square, creasing well.

3 Unfold completely.

4 Fold paper in half into a triangle, creasing well.

5 Fold in half into a triangle again, creasing well.

6 Hold point A (top layer) up straight from dotted line edge.

7 Open sides of this layer by sliding finger inside, and flatten into a diamond.

112

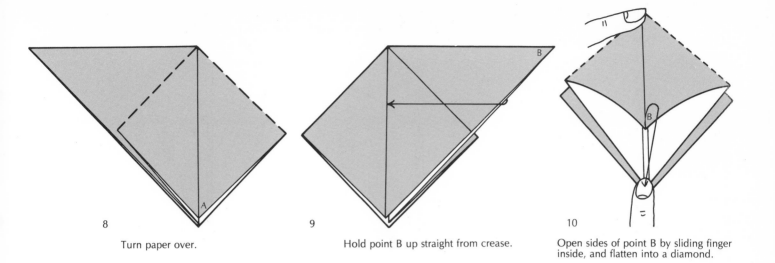

8

Turn paper over.

9

Hold point B up straight from crease.

10

Open sides of point B by sliding finger inside, and flatten into a diamond.

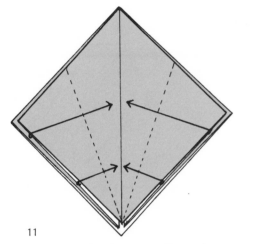

11

Fold top layer edges in to center line as shown.

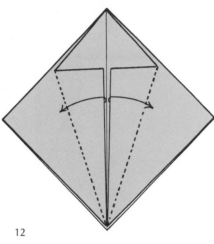

12

Hold center triangles up straight from creases.

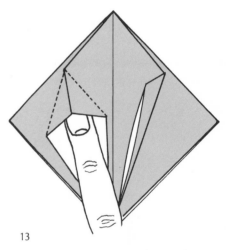

13

Open sides by sliding fingers inside, and flatten into kites.

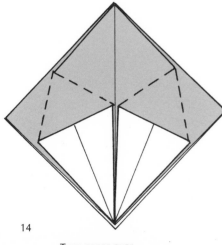

14

Turn paper over, and repeat steps 11–13.

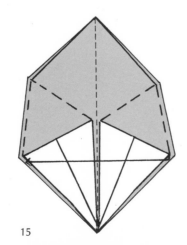

15

Fold top right layer to the left.

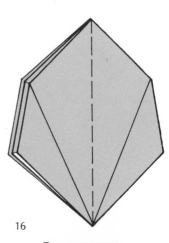

16

Turn paper over, and repeat step 15.

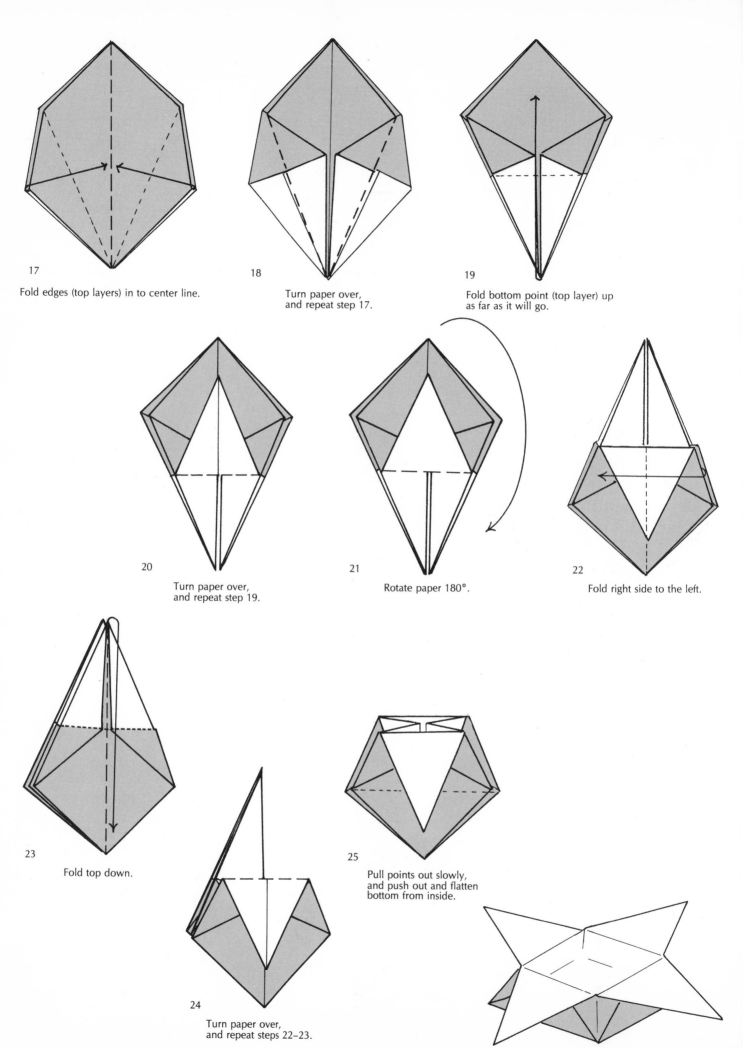

17
Fold edges (top layers) in to center line.

18
Turn paper over,
and repeat step 17.

19
Fold bottom point (top layer) up
as far as it will go.

20
Turn paper over,
and repeat step 19.

21
Rotate paper 180°.

22
Fold right side to the left.

23
Fold top down.

24
Turn paper over,
and repeat steps 22–23.

25
Pull points out slowly,
and push out and flatten
bottom from inside.

BASKET B (4" wide)

MATERIALS: 1 sheet of 6" × 6" paper
(see also p. 128 for suggested color, weight, and size)

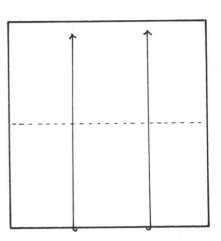

1

Fold paper in half into a rectangle, creasing well.

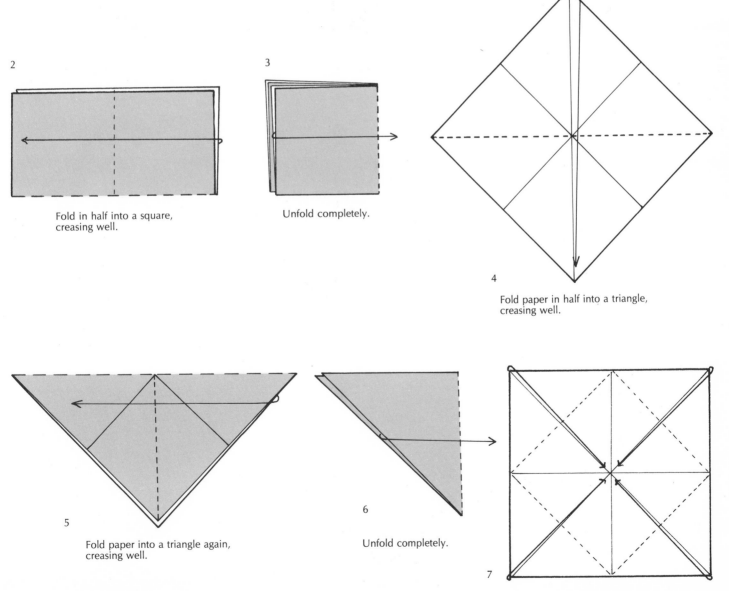

2

Fold in half into a square, creasing well.

3

Unfold completely.

4

Fold paper in half into a triangle, creasing well.

5

Fold paper into a triangle again, creasing well.

6

Unfold completely.

7

Fold corners in to center.

115

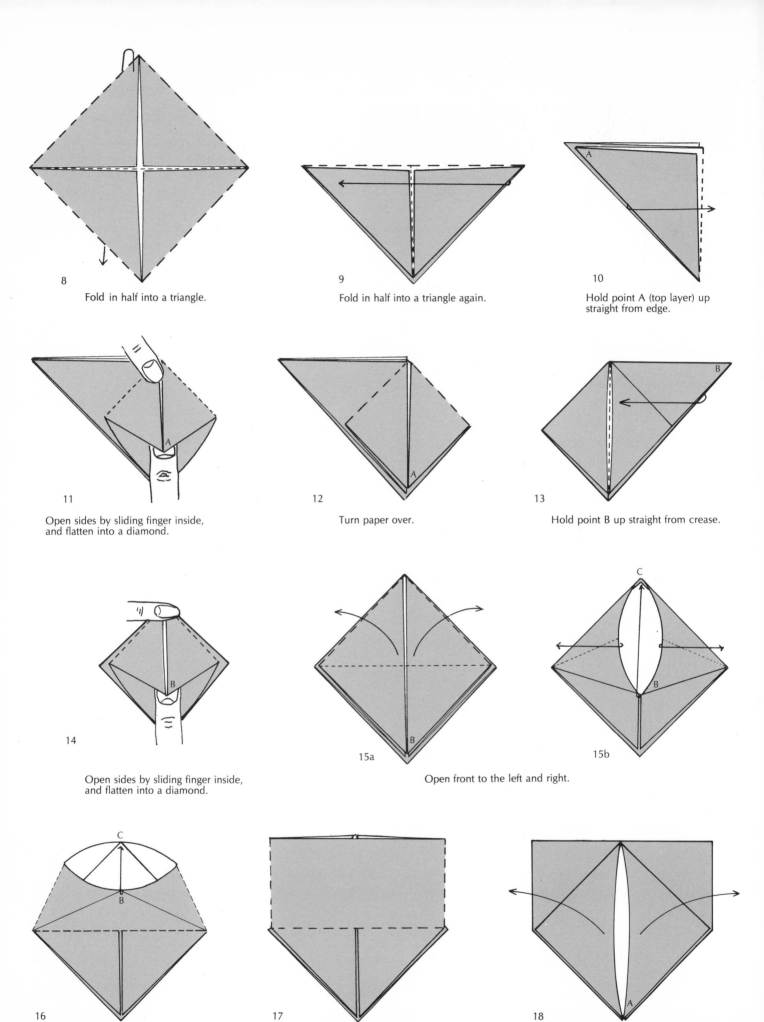

8

Fold in half into a triangle.

9

Fold in half into a triangle again.

10

Hold point A (top layer) up straight from edge.

11

Open sides by sliding finger inside, and flatten into a diamond.

12

Turn paper over.

13

Hold point B up straight from crease.

14

Open sides by sliding finger inside, and flatten into a diamond.

15a

15b

Open front to the left and right.

16

Push point B (top layer) to point C, and flatten into a rectangle.

17

Turn paper over.

18

Open front to the left and right.

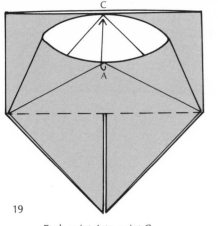

19

Push point A to point C,
and flatten into a rectangle.

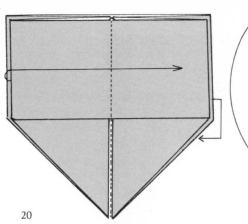

20

Fold top layer of left side to the right
and bottom layer of right side back
and to the left.

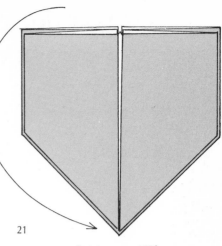

21

Rotate paper 180°

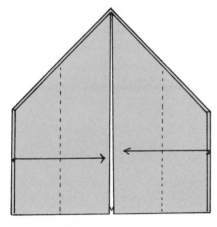

22

Fold edges in to center line.

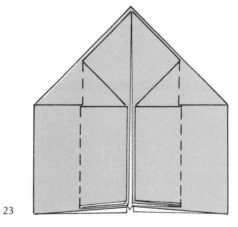

23

Turn paper over, and repeat step 22.

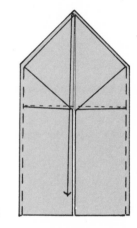

24

Fold top down.

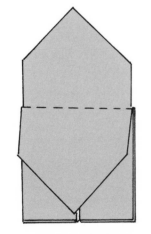

25

Turn paper over, and repeat step 24.

26

Open the basket.

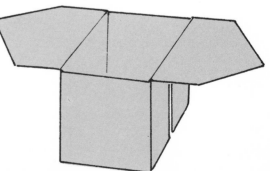

KIMONO (4″ high)

MATERIALS: 1 sheet of 10″ × 14″ paper

(see also p. 124 for suggested color, weight, and size)

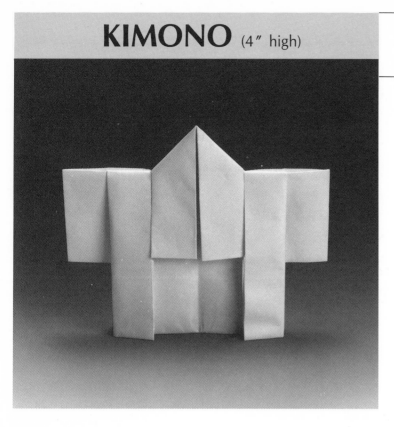

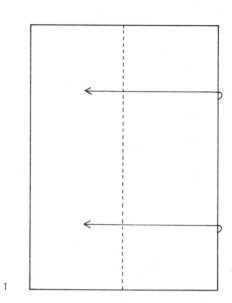

1 Fold paper in half into a rectangle.

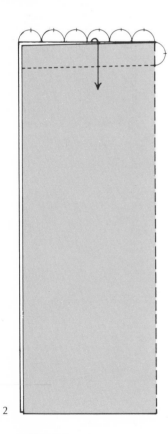

2 Fold top down by an amount equalling one-sixth of its width.

3 Fold top down again.

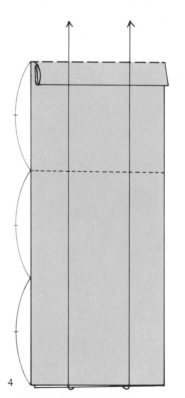

4 Fold bottom up two-thirds of the way.

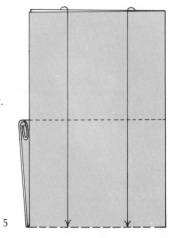

5 Fold new top edge down, towards you.

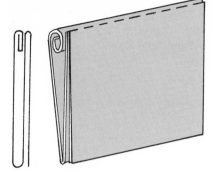

6

Turn paper over.

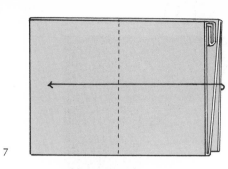

7

Fold in half, creasing well.

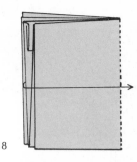

8

Unfold back to diagram 7.

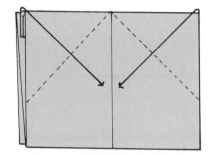

9

Fold corners (top layers) in to center line.

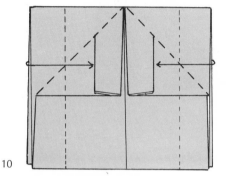

10

Fold sides in to collar's edges.

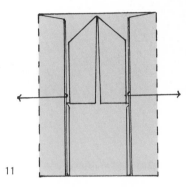

11

Hold sides straight up from edges.

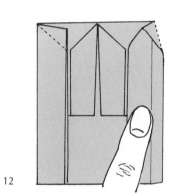

12

Open sides by sliding fingers inside, and flatten.

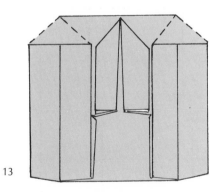

13

Turn paper over.

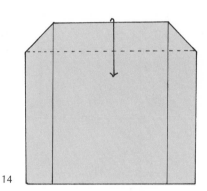

14

Fold top down.

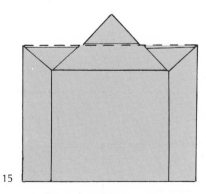

15

Turn paper over.

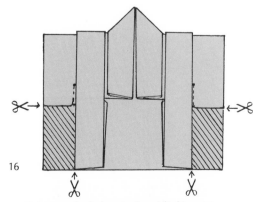

16

Cut away shaded parts. For girl's kimono, cut on dotted lines under arms to make sleeves; do not cut on these dotted lines if it is to be boy's kimono.

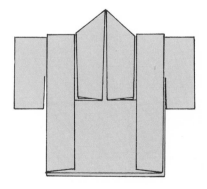

DECORATIVE BOX (2"square)

MATERIALS: 6 sheets of 6" × 6" paper
(see also p. 124 for suggested color, weight, and size)
Glue

1 Fold paper in half into a rectangle, creasing well.

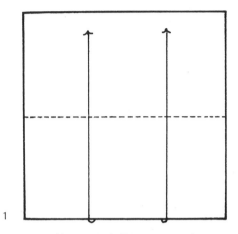

4 Fold right edge to top, creasing well.

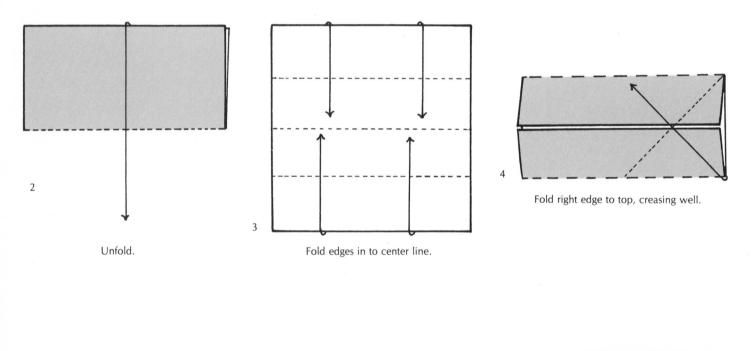

2 Unfold.

3 Fold edges in to center line.

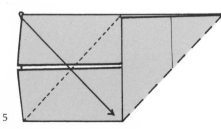

5 Fold left edge to bottom, creasing well.

6 Unfold back to diagram 4, but keep the two small triangles folded (see diagram 7).

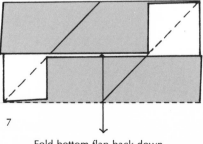

7 Fold bottom flap back down.

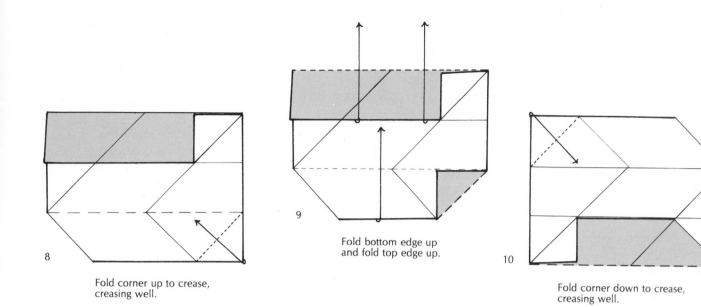

8

Fold corner up to crease,
creasing well.

9

Fold bottom edge up
and fold top edge up.

10

Fold corner down to crease,
creasing well.

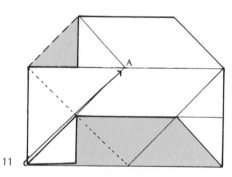

11

Fold corner to point A,
creasing well.

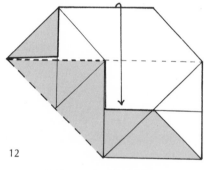

12

Fold top edge back down.

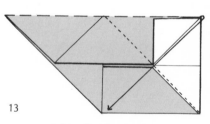

13

Fold right edge to bottom,
creasing well.

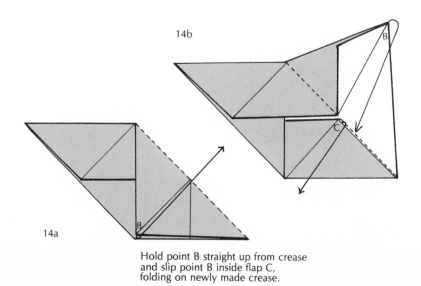

14b

14a

Hold point B straight up from crease
and slip point B inside flap C,
folding on newly made crease.

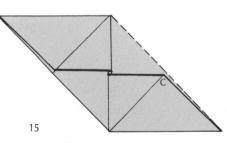

15

Rotate paper, and turn over.

16 Fold sides in, creasing well.

17 Unfold back to step 16, and turn over.

18 Repeat steps 1–17 with five remaining sheets of paper. As you slide flaps into designated slots, as shown, glue each flap.

Note: To hang it from the Christmas tree, use a small needle and fine thread, pull the thread through one corner of cube, tie it in a loop, and hang it from tree.

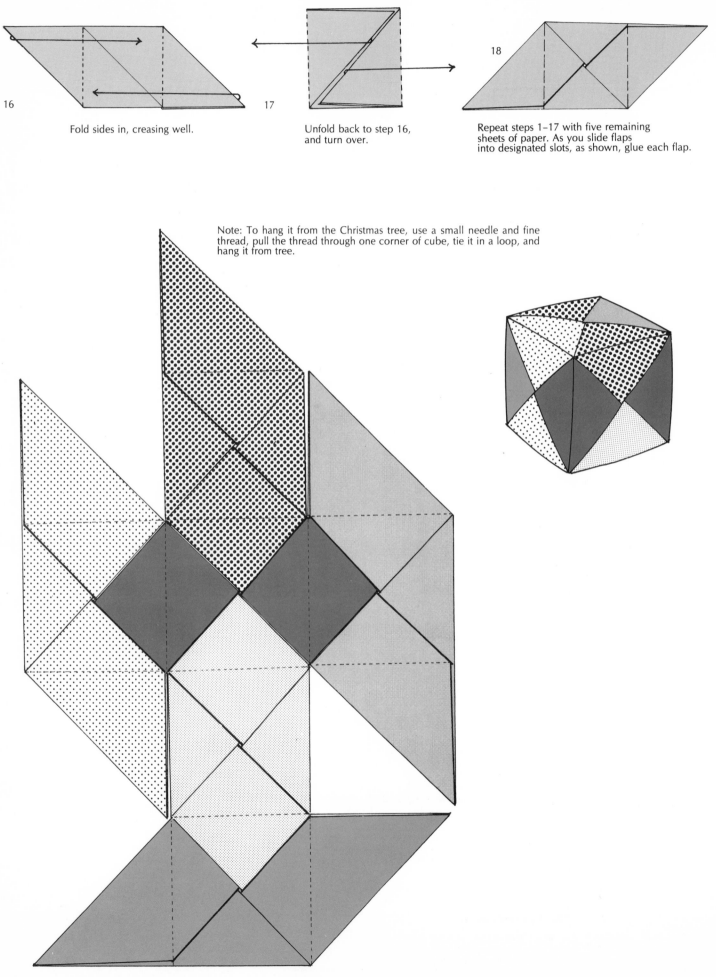

PART 2
CHRISTMAS ARRANGEMENTS

Instructions for the decorations shown in the color plates using
the individual origami designs and a few other materials.

TREE DECORATIONS

Colorful Ornaments

ORNAMENTS: Cranes A (p. 22), cranes B (p. 26), chickens (p. 30), swans (p. 34), doves (p. 36), trees (p. 37), carnations (p. 38), tulips (p. 40), chrysanthemums (p. 42), roses (p. 44), poinsettias (p. 58), Santa Claus (p. 62), angels (p. 78), reindeer B (p. 86), stars (p. 103), bells (p. 106), churches (p. 108), balloon ornaments (p. 110), baskets A (p. 112), kimonos (p. 118), decorative boxes (p. 120).

PAPER: Red, yellow, and white lightweight paper and gold and silver foil in sizes varying from 4″ × 4″ to 8″ × 8″. All sheets should be square except those used for the kimonos, which should be 7″ × 5″. To make sure the Santa Claus is proportioned correctly, suggested paper sizes are: 8″ × 8″ for his body; 3½″ × 3½″ for his boots; and 3¼″ × 3¼″ for his hat.

INSTRUCTIONS: The tree in the photograph (and in Pl. 1) is about six feet high. Ideally you should match the size of the ornaments to the size of the tree you have. In addition, vary the color and the sizes of the paper in order to achieve a colorful balance of decorations.

Trees: You can make large trees by gluing three small trees of different colors back-to-back.

Carnations: Make several carnations, match them by size, and glue them back-to-back two at a time.

Reindeer B: To make the string of reindeer shown in the photograph, arrange several reindeer according to size and string them together with a needle and thread.

Treetop star: Glue red and yellow paper back-to-back and start folding with the yellow side of the paper facing you.

Cranes

ORNAMENTS: Cranes A (p. 22), poinsettias (p. 58), balloon ornaments (p. 110).

PAPER: Light weight paper in white, pastel yellow, pastel blue, and pink, and silver and gold foil in sizes varying from 4″ × 4″ to 8″ × 8″. A larger sheet (13″ × 13″) is necessary only for the topmost poinsettia.

INSTRUCTIONS: The ornaments in the photograph (see also Pl. 2) number some 144 cranes, 7 poinsettias, and 14 balloons. Of course, you may prepare more or fewer, depending on the size of your tree, your other decorations, and individual taste. Note that in the photograph predominantly pastel-shaded paper was chosen intentionally to give a novel and delicate effect, but you may prefer to use other colors as well.

"LACE" CHRISTMAS TREES

MATERIALS			
	TYPE OF PAPER	**NUMBER OF SHEETS**	**DIMENSIONS OF EACH SHEET**
TREES	White, medium weight	1	19″ × 19″
	Blue, medium weight	1	19″ × 19″
	Red, medium weight	1	19″ × 19″
POINSETTIAS	White, light weight	5	3½″ × 3½″
TREETOP POINSETTIAS	White, light weight	1	3½″ × 3½″
	Blue, light weight	1	3½″ × 3½″
	Red, light weight	1	3½″ × 3½″

Other materials: 3 28″ wooden sticks (¼″ diameter);

white, blue, and red paint;

3 flowerpots (or other tree bases);

sand or soil (to fill flowerpots); glue.

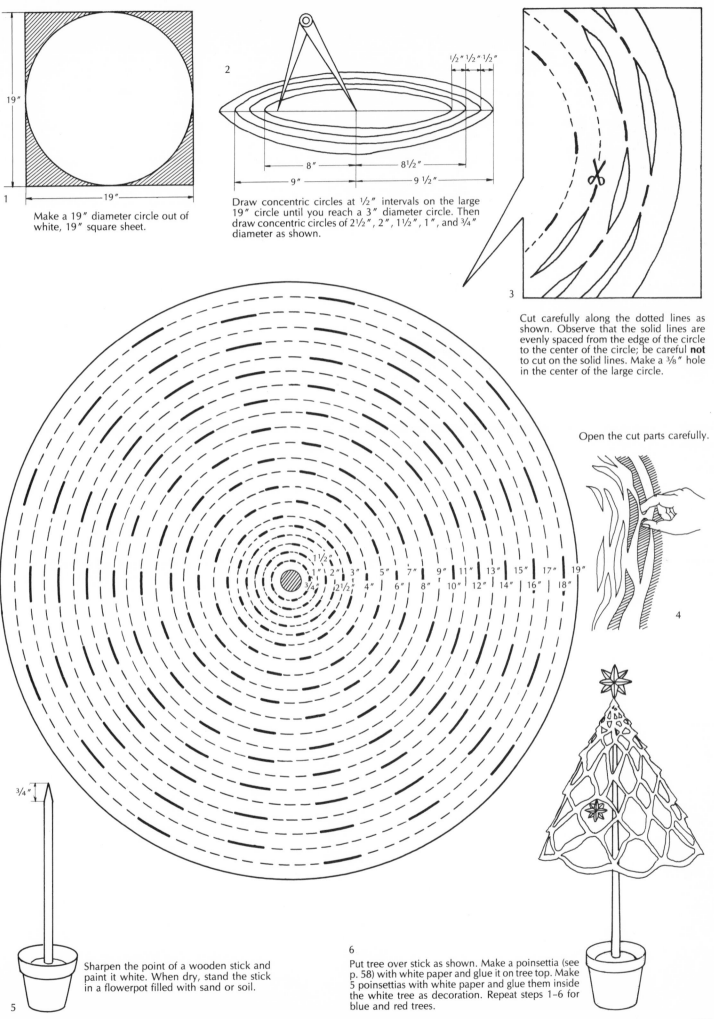

1 Make a 19″ diameter circle out of white, 19″ square sheet.

2 Draw concentric circles at ½″ intervals on the large 19″ circle until you reach a 3″ diameter circle. Then draw concentric circles of 2½″, 2″, 1½″, 1″, and ¾″ diameter as shown.

½″ ½″ ½″
8″ 8½″
9″ 9½″

3 Cut carefully along the dotted lines as shown. Observe that the solid lines are evenly spaced from the edge of the circle to the center of the circle; be careful **not** to cut on the solid lines. Make a ⅜″ hole in the center of the large circle.

Open the cut parts carefully.

4

1½″
1″ 2″ 3″ 5″ 7″ 9″ 11″ 13″ 15″ 17″ 19″
¾″ 2½″ 4″ 6″ 8″ 10″ 12″ 14″ 16″ 18″

¾″

5 Sharpen the point of a wooden stick and paint it white. When dry, stand the stick in a flowerpot filled with sand or soil.

6 Put tree over stick as shown. Make a poinsettia (see p. 58) with white paper and glue it on tree top. Make 5 poinsettias with white paper and glue them inside the white tree as decoration. Repeat steps 1-6 for blue and red trees.

WHITE ORIGAMI TREE

MATERIALS

	TYPE OF PAPER	NUMBER OF SHEETS	DIMENSIONS OF EACH SHEET
ORNAMENTS	White, light weight	59	2″ × 2″
	White, light weight	20	3″ × 3″
	White, light weight	20	3½″ × 3½″
	Gold foil	2	6″ × 6″

Other materials: 8 ft–10 ft of galvanized steel wire;
white adhesive tape (2″–4″ wide);
gold adhesive tape or gold paper;
3 28″ wooden sticks (1/16″ diameter);
1 white lace paper doily (7″ diameter);
1 white flowerpot (5″ diameter, 4″ high);
1 sheet of cardboard (5″ diameter);
sand or soil (to fill flowerpot); 1 1″ nail; white thread; glue.

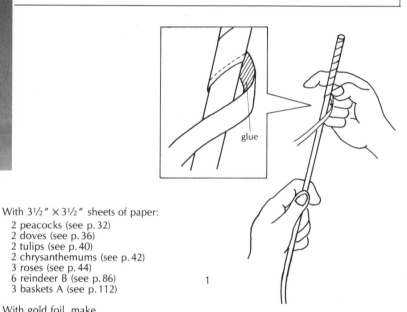

Make the following origami.

With 2″ × 2″ sheets of paper:
3 chickens (see p. 30)
2 peacocks (see p. 32)
2 swans (see p. 34)
20 trees (see p. 37)
4 carnations (see p. 38)
6 chrysanthemums (see p. 42)
16 roses (see p. 44)
4 bells (see p. 106)
2 baskets A (see p. 112)

With 3″ × 3″ sheets of paper:
2 chickens (see p. 30)
1 peacock (see p. 32)
1 swan (see p. 34)
2 carnations (see p. 38)
3 tulips (see p. 40)
1 angel (see p. 78)
2 reindeer B (see p. 86)
6 bells (see p. 106)
2 baskets A (see p. 112)

With 3½″ × 3½″ sheets of paper:
2 peacocks (see p. 32)
2 doves (see p. 36)
2 tulips (see p. 40)
2 chrysanthemums (see p. 42)
3 roses (see p. 44)
6 reindeer B (see p. 86)
3 baskets A (see p. 112)

With gold foil, make
2 poinsettias (see p. 58)

1

Wrap galvanized steel wire with white tape in an even spiral, with the edges of each coil slightly overlapping.

Stretch the wire little by little

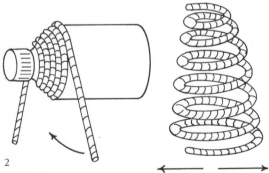 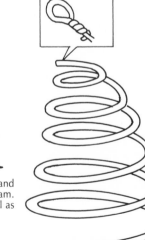

2

Wrap wire around a bottle as shown. Take away the bottle and stretch the wire carefully to form the shape shown in diagram. Make a small circle with the end of the wire to hold a nail as shown.

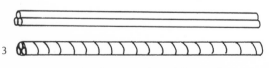

3

Wrap the three wooden sticks together with white tape as in step 1.

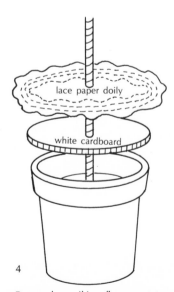

4

Put sand or soil in a flower pot, top with thick cardboard and then lace paper. Stick the pole in the center.

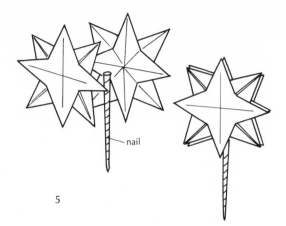

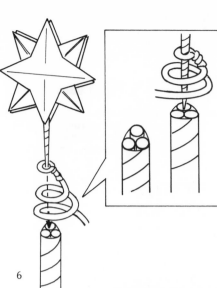

5

Wrap nail with gold tape or paper. Apply glue to the front of two poinsettias. Put the nail between poinsettias and glue them face-to-face.

6

Attach the spiral wire to the pole, and nail into top of pole as shown.

7

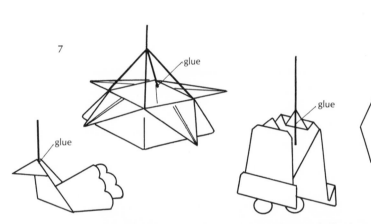

Glue thread to the origami as shown. Glue two bells of same size back-to-back, placing the thread between them. Do the same with trees, carnations, and chrysanthemums.

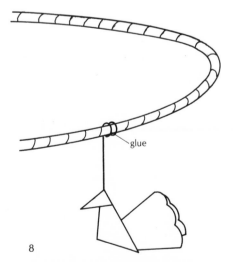

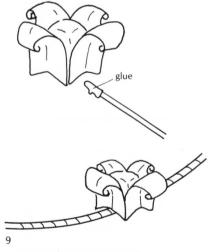

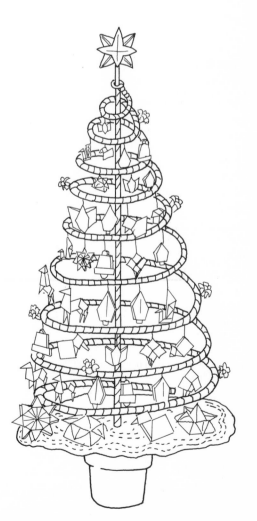

8

Attach all origami except the roses to the wire, winding the thread around the wire several times, and then applying glue to the thread.

9

Apply glue to the back of the roses and glue them directly to the wire anywhere you like.

NATIVITY SCENE

Make Mary (see p. 69), infant Jesus (see p. 72), three Wise Men with capes (see p. 75), three horses (see p. 93), three camels (see p. 96), a cradle-manger for Jesus (see p. 102), and a manger. Make a poinsettia (see p. 58) with gold foil for the star. Make two gifts (basket B, see p. 115) with yellow-green and orange paper. (You may wish to add another gift for your scene.)

MATERIALS

	TYPE OF PAPER	NUMBER OF SHEETS	DIMENSIONS OF EACH SHEET
INFANT JESUS	Blue, light weight	1	2″ × 2″
MARY	Pink, light weight	1	6″ × 6″
THREE WISE MEN	Bright colored, light weight	3	5¼″ × 5¼″
CAPES (FOR WISE MEN)	Bright decorative, light weight	3	8″ × 8″
GIFTS	Yellow-green, light weight	1	2⅜″ × 2⅜″
	Orange, light weight	1	2⅜″ × 2⅜″
HORSES AND CAMELS	Beige or brown, medium weight	6	7″ × 7″
CRADLE-MANGER	Yellow, light weight	1	2¾″ × 2¾″
MANGER	Red, light weight	1	4¼″ × 4¼″
MANGER STAND	Black, medium weight	2	1″ × 1″
	Black, medium weight	1	1″ × ⅛″
STAR	Gold foil	1	5½″ × 5½″
STAND	Cardboard	2	20″ × 16″
GROUND	Dark green, light weight	1	22″ × 18″
BACKGROUND	White or blue, light weight	1	22″ × 17″
LARGE STABLE	Black, medium weight	1	7½″ × 13″
SMALL STABLE	Black, medium weight	1	7″ × 10″
LARGE STABLE WALL AND FLOOR	Gold foil	1	6½″ × 12″
SMALL STABLE WALL AND FLOOR	Gold foil	1	6″ × 9″

Other materials: wide adhesive tape; glue.

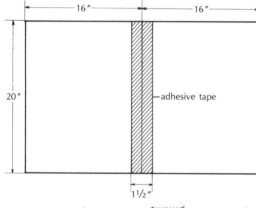

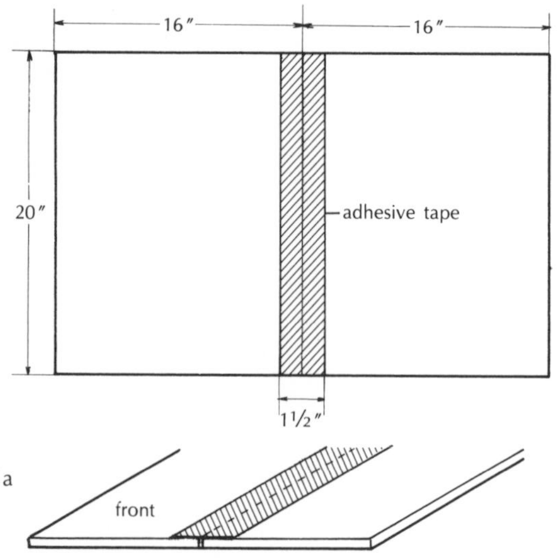

1a

To make stand, attach two 20″ × 16″ sheets of card-board together, applying tape to the shaded part.

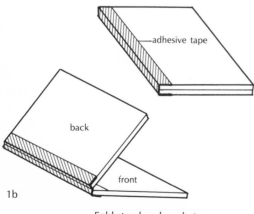

1b

Fold stand and apply tape for back hinge as shown.

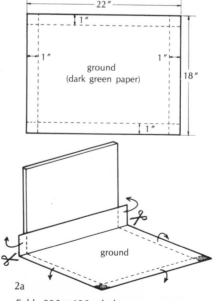

2a

Fold 22″ × 18″ dark green paper as shown. Glue it to the stand for the ground, cutting away the shaded parts. Fold the excess parts back and under, and glue them down.

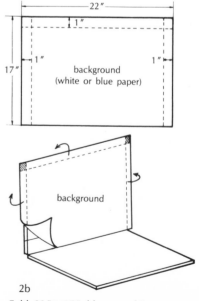

2b

Fold 22″ × 17″ blue or white paper as shown. Glue it to the background, cutting off the shaded parts. Fold the excess parts back and glue them down. If you use white paper for the background, paint it as you like before gluing.

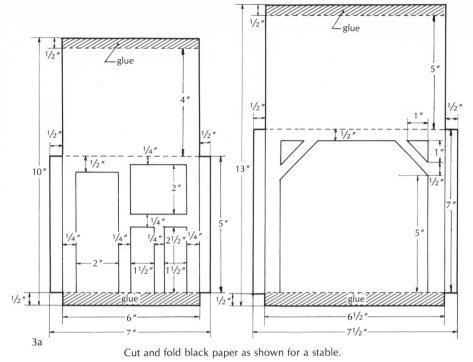

3a

Cut and fold black paper as shown for a stable.

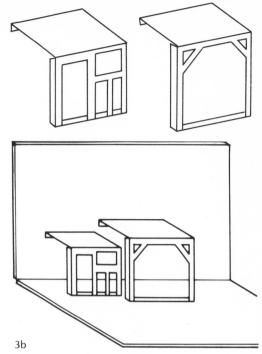

3b

Prior to affixing the stable to stage, position the two parts of the stable a little left of the center of the stand.

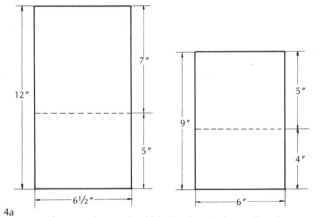

4a

Glue two sheets of gold foil to the shaded wall and floor of the stand.

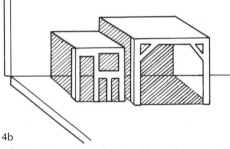

4b

Glue the two parts of the stable to the stand; be careful to glue them straight.

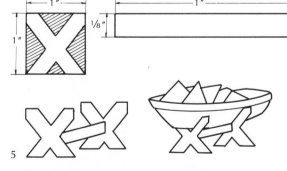

5

To make the manger stand, cut shaded part out of two 1″ squares of black medium weight paper. Glue 1″ × 1/8″ strip of black medium weight paper between them as shown. Put the smaller cradle-manger on the manger stand.

Put the larger manger and three horses in the left stable, and in the right stable put Mary and the infant Jesus in the small manger. Attach baskets to two (or three) Wise Men. Put the three camels outside stable, and glue star in background.

6

SANTA CLAUS MOBILE

MATERIALS			
	TYPE OF PAPER	NUMBER OF SHEETS	DIMENSIONS OF EACH SHEET
BODY	Red, medium weight	1	10" × 10"
HAT	Red, medium weight	1	3⅓" × 3⅓"
HAT CUFF	White, medium weight	1	1⅓" × ⅜"
HAT'S POMPOM	White, medium weight	1	⅜" diameter
PANTS	Red, medium weight	1	4" × 3"
BELLY	Red, medium weight	1	4" diameter
BOOTS	Black, medium weight	2	3⅜" × 3⅜"
BEARD	White, medium weight	1	3⅛" × 3⅜"
BELT	White, medium weight	1	9¼" × ½"
CUFFS	White, medium weight	2	1½" × ¼"
POINSETTIA	Gold foil	1	2⅜" × 2⅜"

Other materials: red thread and needle; glue.

Begin to make Santa Claus's body (see p. 62) with red paper, stop at step 20, and turn paper over. Make Santa's hat. Make his boots with black paper. Make a poinsettia (see p. 58) with gold foil.

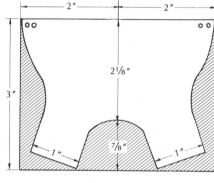

1

Cut Santa's pants out as shown. On 4" circle of red paper draw five concentric circles at intervals of ⅜" and cut spiral as shown. Make four holes in pants and spiral circle as shown.

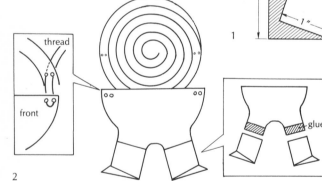

2

Thread needle, and pass thread through the holes in Santa's pants and the circle as shown. Glue Santa's boots to the shaded part of the pants.

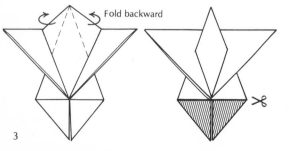

Fold backward

3

Fold Santa's head as shown and cut off the shaded part.

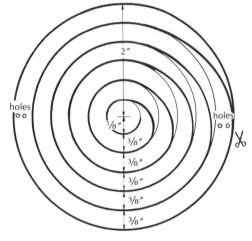

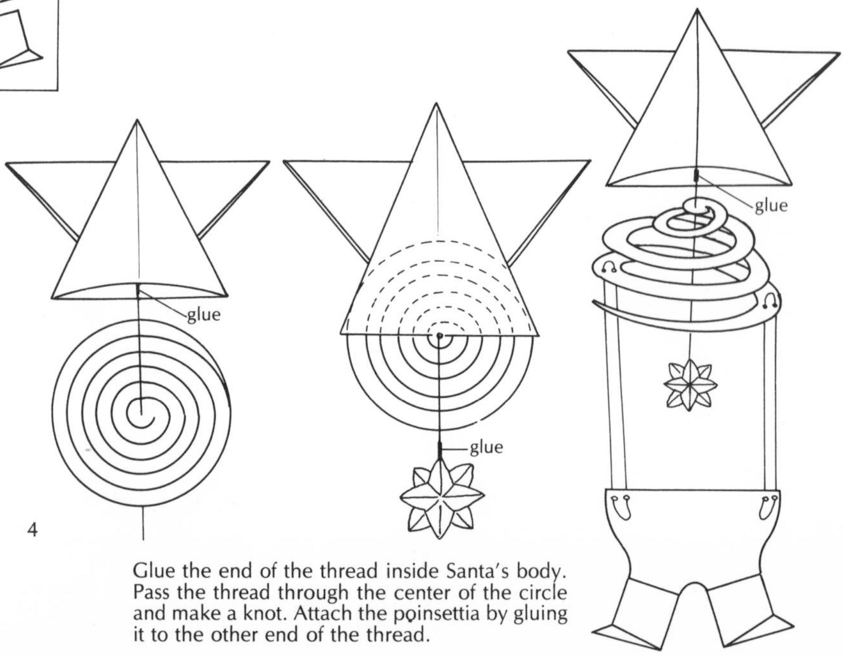

4

Glue the end of the thread inside Santa's body. Pass the thread through the center of the circle and make a knot. Attach the poinsettia by gluing it to the other end of the thread.

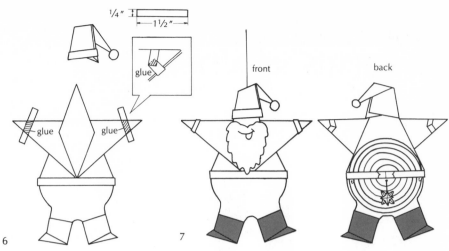

5
Cut two slits on 9¼" × ½" white, medium weight paper as shown. Glue this belt to shaded part of Santa's body, crossing it behind the body.

6
Glue on Santa Claus's beard, hat, and the cuffs of his gloves.

7
Hang the completed Santa by a thread.

DOVE MOBILE

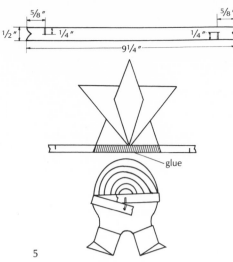

MATERIALS			
	TYPE OF PAPER	**NUMBER OF SHEETS**	**DIMENSIONS OF EACH SHEET**
DOVES	Gold foil	2	6" × 6"
	Gold foil	4	4¾" × 4¾"
	Gold foil	3	3" × 3"
	Gold foil	1	2¼" × 2¼"
	Purple foil	1	6" × 6"
	Silver foil	1	4¾" × 4¾"
	Silver foil	3	3" × 3"
	Green foil	1	4¾" × 4¾"
	Green foil	1	2¼" × 2¼"
	Blue foil	1	6" × 6"
	Red foil	1	4¾" × 4¾"
	Orange foil	1	4¾" × 4¾"
PERCHES	Black, medium weight	2	5½" diameter
	Black, medium weight	4	4¼" diameter
	Black, medium weight	3	3" diameter
	Black, medium weight	1	2¼" diameter

Other materials: 1 12½" galvanized steel wire; 1 8" galvanized steel wire; 4 7" galvanized steel wires; gold adhesive tape; gold cord; glue.

Glue gold foil back-to-back with other colored sheets in corresponding sizes. Make ten doves (see p. 36) of various sizes. Be sure to begin folding each dove with the gold side facing down.

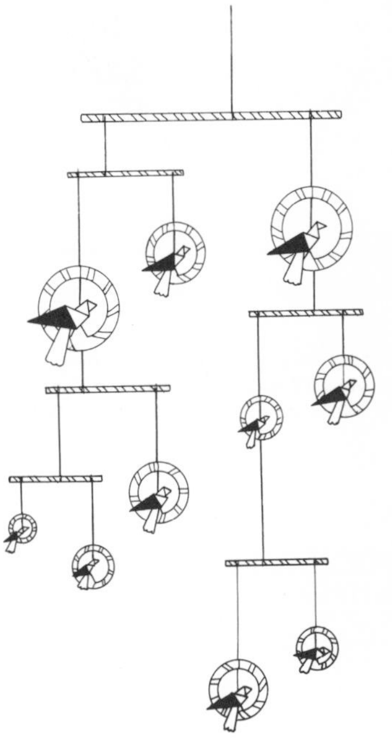

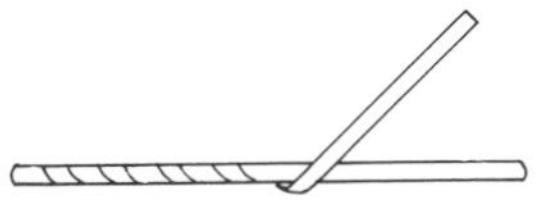

3
Wrap galvanized steel wire with gold tape.

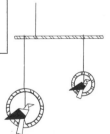

4
Tie cords from two perches to ends of a section of wire and find the point where two perches balance evenly; tie and glue the cord at that point. Continue to construct the mobile as shown, balancing perches at each step. Be sure to begin to construct the mobile from the bottom up.

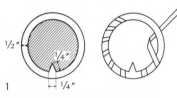

1
Cut the shaded part out of black paper circles to make circular perches. Wrap the circles with gold tape at regular intervals.

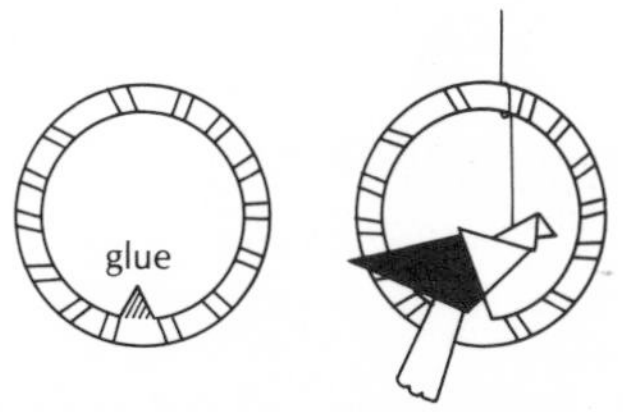

2
Glue a bird to the raised point on the inside of the perch. Repeat with remaining birds and perches. Glue the end of gold cord to the head of each bird, and tie the cord to the top of each perch, leaving 8"–12" of cord.

SANTA CLAUS AND HIS REINDEER

MATERIALS

	TYPE OF PAPER	NUMBER OF SHEETS	DIMENSIONS OF EACH SHEET
BODY	Red, medium weight	1	7″ × 7″
HAT	Red, medium weight	1	3″ × 3″
HAT CUFF	White, medium weight	1	1¼″ × ⅜″
HAT'S POMPOM	White, medium weight	1	⅜″ diameter
BOOTS	Black, medium weight	2	3½″ × 3½″
BAG	White, light weight	1	8⅝″ × 8⅝″
BEARD	White, medium weight	1	1⅛″ × 1½″
REINDEER	Green dotted, medium weight	7	9″ × 9″
ANTLERS	Black, medium weight	7	3½″ × 1″
HARNESSES	Black, medium weight	7	7″ × ⅛″
SLEIGH	Silver, medium weight	1	10″ × 10″
SLEIGH RUNNERS	Black, medium weight	2	6″ × 2″
SLEIGH DECORATION	Black, medium weight	1	1½″ × ¾″

Other materials: 1 10″ long white floral wire; 12½″ of white ribbon; 40″ of silver cord; glue.

Make Santa Claus (see p. 62). Make seven reindeer B (see p. 86) and a sleigh (see p. 102). For Santa's bag, make a persimmon (see p. 52) with white, light weight paper.

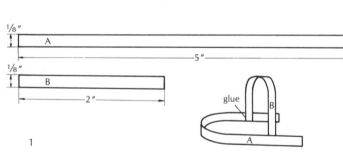

1

Make reindeer harnesses with black, medium weight paper as shown.

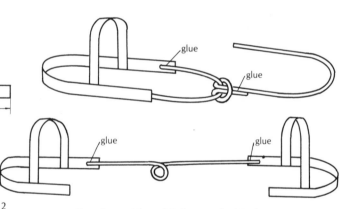

2

For reins, cut three 6″ silver cords. Attach each 6″ cord to each of three pairs of harnesses as shown. Glue the remaining 22″ silver cord to harness of lead reindeer as shown.

3

Put harnesses on reindeer.

4

Fold 3½″ × 1″ piece of black paper in half and cut out a pair of antlers. Glue the antlers behind the head of a reindeer. Repeat with the six other reindeer.

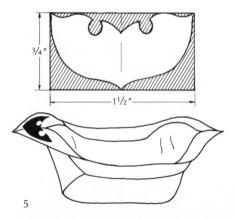

5

Cut sleigh decoration from 1½″ × ¾″ black paper and glue on one end of sleigh.

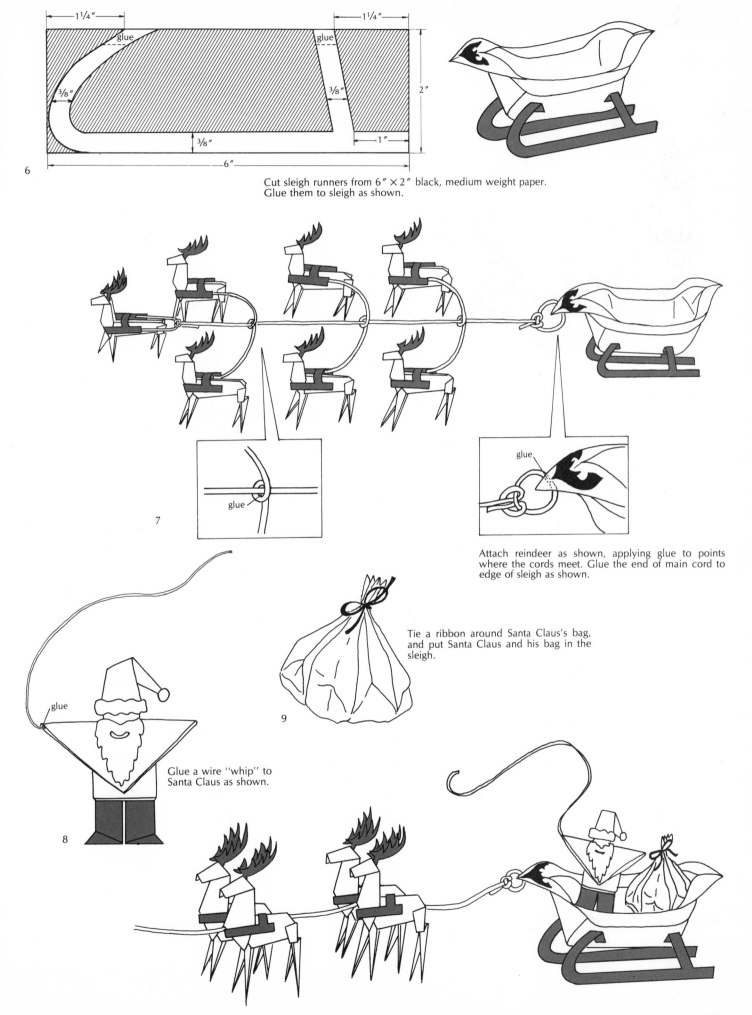

6 Cut sleigh runners from 6″ × 2″ black, medium weight paper.
Glue them to sleigh as shown.

7

Attach reindeer as shown, applying glue to points
where the cords meet. Glue the end of main cord to
edge of sleigh as shown.

9 Tie a ribbon around Santa Claus's bag,
and put Santa Claus and his bag in the
sleigh.

8 Glue a wire "whip" to
Santa Claus as shown.

CHRISTMAS WREATHS

Poinsettia

Make eight poinsettias (see p. 58).

(see p. 58)

MATERIALS			
	TYPE OF PAPER	**NUMBER OF SHEETS**	**DIMENSIONS OF EACH SHEET**
POINSETTIAS	Red, light weight	8	6″ × 6″
LEAVES	Green, medium weight	150–200	2¾″ × 2″

Other materials: 150–200 4″ long green floral wires;
10 ft of green floral wire; 8″ of green cord;
styrofoam wreath base (12″ diameter);
5 ft of black and beige striped ribbon;
8 adhesive red stars; glue.

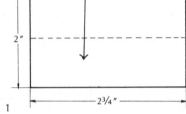

1. Make a holly leaf by folding a piece of green paper in half. Cut off the shaded part. Score the dotted lines with blunt scissors.

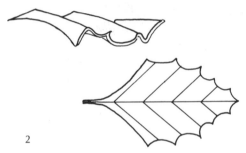

2. Fold in "accordion" creases as shown and then unfold completely.

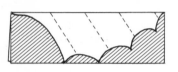

3. Glue 4″ floral wire to a leaf. Repeat steps 1–3 with remaining green paper and wire.

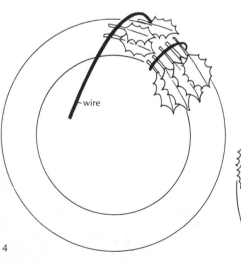

4. Affix holly leaf stems onto the wreath base, by sticking four or five holly leaves into the base at one time and binding them onto the base tightly with wire as shown.

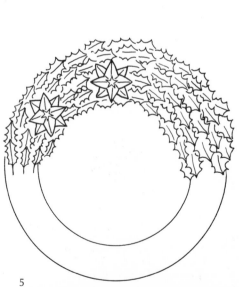

5. Glue the poinsettias onto the leaves. Apply red adhesive stars to the centers of the poinsettias.

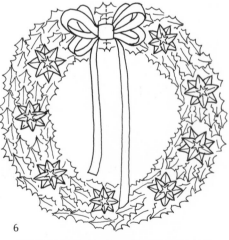

6. Tie a bow with black and beige striped ribbon and attach it to the wreath with green cord. Using wire, cord, or double-adhesive tape, hang the wreath on a door or in a window.

Persimmon

MATERIALS			
	TYPE OF PAPER	**NUMBER OF SHEETS**	**DIMENSIONS OF EACH SHEET**
PERSIMMONS	Gold striped foil	30	3″ × 3″
	Gold striped foil	20	4¼″ × 4¼″
	Gold striped foil	20	6″ × 6″
Other materials: 140 1½″ long floral wires; 1 6″ long floral wire; styrofoam wreath base (12″ diameter); 3 ft–5 ft of gold ribbon; glue.			

Make seventy persimmons (see p. 52) with gold foil.

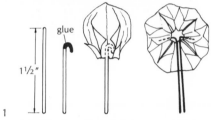

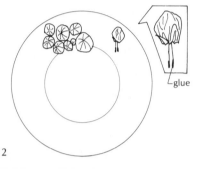

1
Bend the tips of two wires, apply glue to the ends, and insert both wires into the hole in one persimmon.

2
Apply glue to the other ends of the wires and stick the persimmon into the wreath base. Repeat steps 1 and 2 with the other sixty-nine persimmons and the remaining wire.

3
Tie a bow with gold ribbon. Slip wire through the back of the bow. Apply glue to the tip of the wire and stick the wire into wreath base. Using wire, cord, or double-adhesive tape, hang the wreath on a door or in a window.

White Swan

MATERIALS			
	TYPE OF PAPER	**NUMBER OF SHEETS**	**DIMENSIONS OF EACH SHEET**
WHITE SWANS	White, medium weight	28	5″ × 5″
BLUE SWANS	Blue, medium weight	2	4″ × 4″
Other materials: 28 straight pins; 1 12″ long white floral wire; styrofoam wreath base (8″ diameter); 15–20 adhesive gold stars; 5 adhesive red stars; glue.			

Make twenty-eight swans with white paper and two swans with blue paper (see p. 34). Open swan's wing as shown and bring point A to point B, flattening the swan. Repeat with remaining swans.

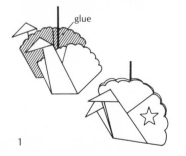

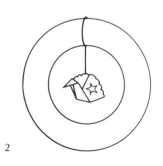

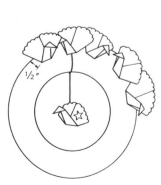

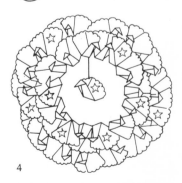

1
Place the white floral wire between the two blue swans and glue them back-to-back. Apply a gold adhesive star to each wing.

2
Wrap the wire with the blue swans around the wreath base once so that the swans hang in the center of the wreath.

3
With pins, attach sixteen white swans to the wreath base ½″ from the edge.

4
Attach the remaining twelve white swans to the wreath base. Apply gold and red stars to the swans at random. Using wire, cord, or double-adhesive tape, hang the wreath on a door or in a window.

Crane

MATERIALS			
	TYPE OF PAPER	**NUMBER OF SHEETS**	**DIMENSIONS OF EACH SHEET**
CRANES	Gold, light weight	3	4¾″ × 4¾″
	Gold, light weight	9	3½″ × 3½″
	Red, light weight	3	4¾″ × 4¾″
	Red, light weight	9	3½″ × 3½″
Other materials: natural or artificial evergreen wreath (12″ diameter); 24 1¾″ long green floral wires; 3 ft–5 ft of red ribbon; 1 6″ long green floral wire; glue.			

Make twenty-four cranes (see p. 22) with gold and red paper.

1

Apply glue to the end of a 1¾″ wire and stick it into the hole underneath the crane. Repeat with remaining cranes and wire.

2

glue

Apply glue to the other end of each wire and stick cranes into the wreath base.

3

glue

Tie a bow with red ribbon. Slip wire through the back of the bow. Apply glue to the end of the wire and stick it into the wreath base. Using wire or cord, hang the wreath on a door or in a window.

HOLIDAY GREETING CARDS

Spiral Loop Card

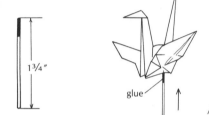

MATERIALS			
	TYPE OF PAPER	**NUMBER OF SHEETS**	**DIMENSIONS OF EACH SHEET**
CARD	Yellow, medium weight	1	16″ × 6½″
POINSETTIA	Red, light weight	1	2½″ × 2½″
Other materials: about 10 red adhesive stars; glue.			

Make a poinsettia (see p. 58) with red paper.

1

Fold yellow paper as shown, and then carefully cut along the spiral line.

16″

6½″

glue

¼″

1″ 5″ 5″ 4¾″ ¼″

2

glue

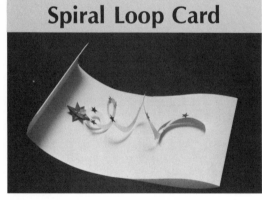

Fold ¼″ of the right edge to the inside. Apply glue to this narrow right panel and fold it over so it adheres along the left fold of the center panel. Pull out the center part of the spiral and glue it to the center of left panel.

3

Glue poinsettia to the end of spiral and decorate with red adhesive stars.

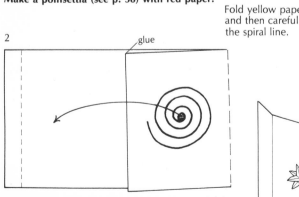

4

Fold the card as shown.

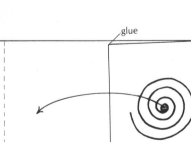

Birdcage Card

MATERIALS

	TYPE OF PAPER	NUMBER OF SHEETS	DIMENSIONS OF EACH SHEET
CARD	White, medium weight	1	12″ × 10″
	Green, medium weight	1	6″ × 4¾″
LABEL	White, medium weight	1	3″ × ¾″
DOVE	White, light weight	1	4¾″ × 4¾″
BELLS	Gold foil	4	2¾″ × 2¾″
PERCH	Dark brown, light weight	1	4″ × 2½″
PERCH BASE	White, medium weight	1	4″ × 2½″

Other materials: glue.

Make a dove (see p. 36) with white, light weight paper, and make four bells (see p. 106) with gold foil.

Cut shaded part of white, medium weight paper as shown to make cage design.

1

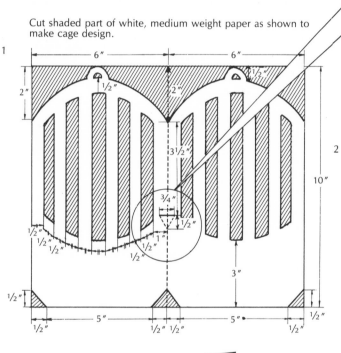

2

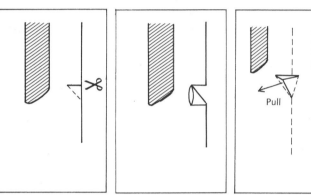

Fold the card in half and cut ⅜″ horizontally as shown. Fold on the small dotted line as shown and then unfold. Open the card and pull the triangle inside the card along the dotted line.

3

Glue 4″ × 2½″ dark brown paper to 4″ × 2½″ white medium weight paper. Cut out a perch as shown.

4

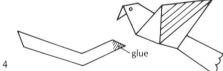

Glue your favorite colored paper to the bird's wing or paint the wing. Glue the shaded part of perch to inside bird's body.

5

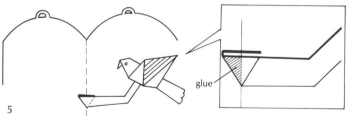

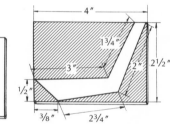

Glue the shaded part of perch to the card as shown.

6

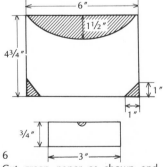

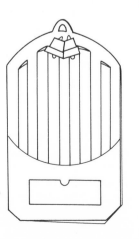

Cut green paper as shown and glue it to the front of the card. Cut a label out of 3″ × ¾″ piece of white, medium weight paper and glue it on the green paper. Glue two bells to the top of the card.

7

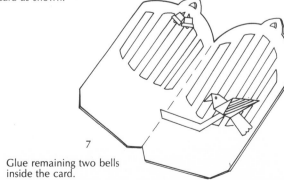

Glue remaining two bells inside the card.

Praying Hands Cards

Orange

MATERIALS			
	TYPE OF PAPER	NUMBER OF SHEETS	DIMENSIONS OF EACH SHEET
CARD	Orange, medium weight	1	6¾" × 7"
CHRYSAN-THEMUM	White, light weight	1	2¾" × 2¾"
Other materials: glue.			

Make a chrysanthemum (see p. 42) with white paper.

1. Following the pattern for the white card below, cut a hand-shaped card out of orange, medium weight paper. The sizes for this orange card are indicated in parentheses.

2. Glue chrysanthemum in the center of the inside of the hand-shaped card.

Make a chrysanthemum (see p. 42), with gold foil.

1. Cut a hand-shaped card out of white, medium weight paper.

2. Glue the chrysanthemum on the inside of the card as shown.

3. Glue pieces of colored, medium weight paper together one by one to make a circular rainbow as shown. Cut out shaded center part.

White

MATERIALS			
	TYPE OF PAPER	NUMBER OF SHEETS	DIMENSIONS OF EACH SHEET
CARD	White, medium weight	1	8½" × 8¾"
CHRYSAN-THEMUM	Gold foil	1	3¼" × 3¼"
RAINBOW	Yellow, medium weight	1	2¼" diameter
	Orange, medium weight	1	2" diameter
	Pink, medium weight	1	1¾" diameter
	Red, medium weight	1	1½" diameter
	Purple, medium weight	1	1¼" diameter
Other materials: glue.			

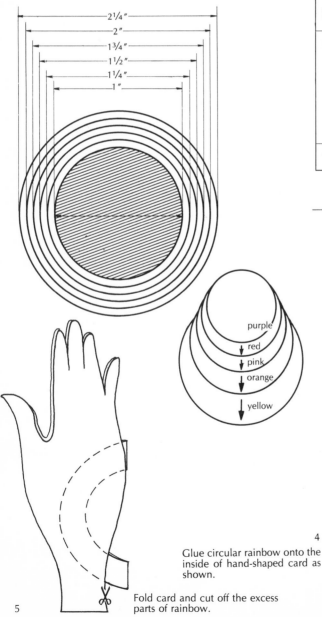

purple
red
pink
orange
yellow

4

Glue circular rainbow onto the inside of hand-shaped card as shown.

Fold card and cut off the excess parts of rainbow.

5

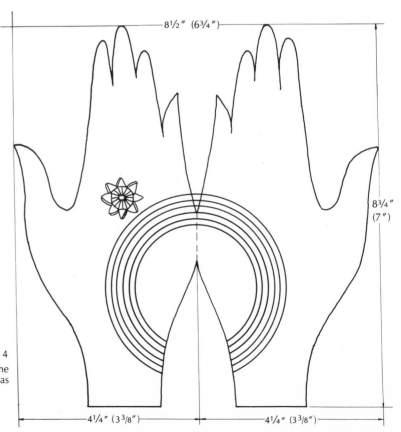

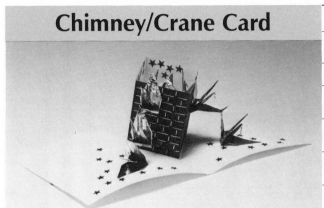

Chimney/Crane Card

MATERIALS			
	TYPE OF PAPER	**NUMBER OF SHEETS**	**DIMENSIONS OF EACH SHEET**
CRANES	Gold foil	8	4¼″ × 4¼″
CARD	White, medium weight	1	14″ × 8″
CHIMNEY (INSIDE)	Black, medium weight	1	4¼″ × 12¼″
CHIMNEY (OUTSIDE)	Brown, light weight	1	3¾″ × 12″

Other materials: about 30 red adhesive stars; glue.

Make eight cranes A (see p. 22) with gold foil.

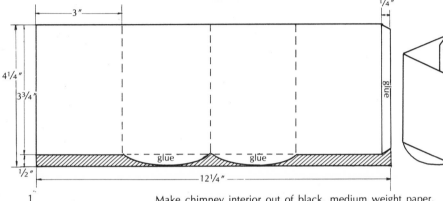

1

Make chimney interior out of black, medium weight paper. Cut out the shaded part from the bottom edge. Fold as shown. Apply glue to the right edge and shape as shown.

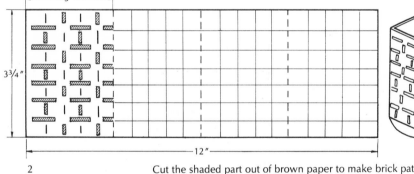

2

Cut the shaded part out of brown paper to make brick pattern for the outside of the chimney. Glue the paper onto the chimney interior base. (For step 1, you may prefer to use brown cardboard, draw brick pattern directly on it, and eliminate step 2.)

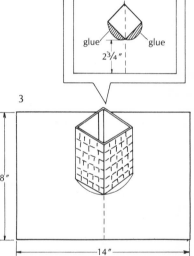

3

Glue the bottom of chimney flaps onto center of card which has been folded in half. Be sure that the fold of the card and the diagonal line of the chimney are aligned.

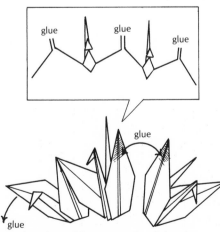

4

Make a line of four cranes by gluing the tips of their wings together as shown. Make another line with the remaining four cranes.

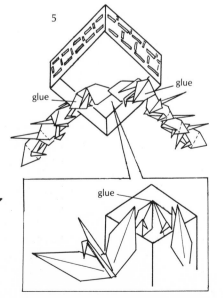

5

6

Put one crane of each group into the chimney and glue their wings onto the inside wall of the chimney. Glue together the other wings of these two cranes. Arrange remaining cranes on the card as shown and glue appropriate cranes securely to the exterior chimney wall and the card itself.

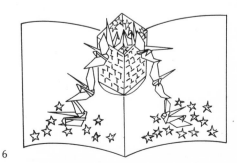

Apply adhesive stars to the card.

Santa Claus Card

MATERIALS

	TYPE OF PAPER	NUMBER OF SHEETS	DIMENSIONS OF EACH SHEET
BODY	Red, light weight	1	7½″ × 7½″
HAT	Red, light weight	1	3″ × 3″
HAT CUFF	White, light weight	1	1¼″ × ⅜″
HAT'S POMPOM	White, light weight	1	⅜″ in diameter
BOOTS	Black, light weight	2	4″ × 4″
BEARD	White, light weight	1	3″ × 1¾″
MOUSTACHE	White, light weight	1	1½″ × ¾″
BAG	White, medium weight	1	5″ × 4¼″
BELT	White, light weight	1	3″ × ¼″
CUFFS	White, light weight	2	1½″ × ¼″
CARD	White, medium weight	1	12″ × 8″
CARD FRONT	White, medium weight	1	6″ × 8″
FIREPLACE	Brown, medium weight	1	12″ × 8″
FIRE GRATE	Silver foil	1	7½″ × 3¼″
CHIMNEY	Dark brown, light weight	1	6″ × 8″

Other materials: glue.

Make a Santa Claus and his hat with red paper, and boots with black paper (see p. 62).

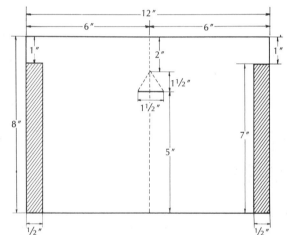

1

Make the card with white, medium weight paper and cut out the shaded part· as shown.

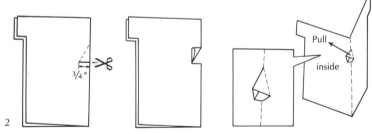

2

Fold the card in half and cut ¾″ horizontally as shown. Fold on the small dotted line as shown and then unfold. Open the card and pull the triangle inside the card along the dotted line.

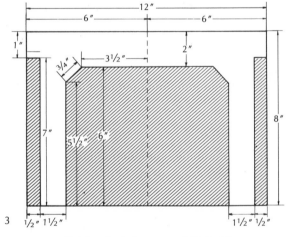

3

Cut the shaded part out of 12″ × 8″ brown paper to make a fireplace.

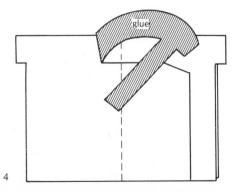

4

Glue the fireplace inside the card base.

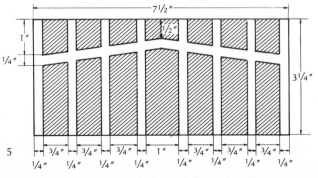

5

Cut out the shaded part of silver foil to make a fire grate.

140

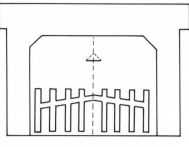

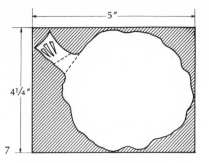

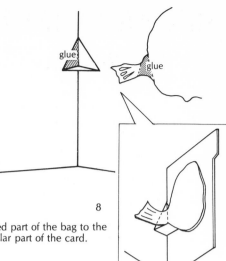

6

Glue the fire grate inside the card as shown; leave the third and fourth posts unglued, in order to insert one of Santa's legs later.

7

Cut Santa's bag out of the 5″ × 4¼″ white, medium weight paper. Make two folds as shown.

8

Glue the shaded part of the bag to the shaded triangular part of the card.

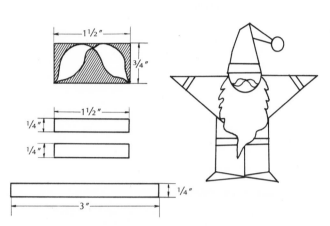

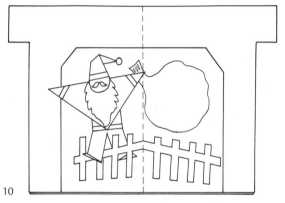

9

Cut Santa's mustache out of 1½″ × ¾″ white medium weight paper and cut cuffs and belt. Glue the mustache, cuffs, and belt to Santa Claus.

10

Glue Santa Claus onto the card as shown.

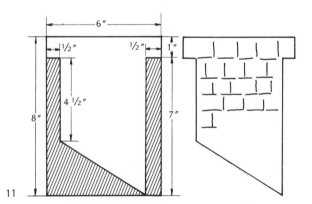

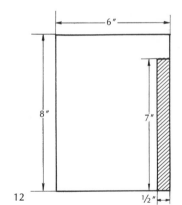

11

Cut the shaded part out of 6″ × 8″ dark brown paper to make a chimney. Draw a brick pattern onto the paper.

12

Cut the shaded part out of 6″ × 8″ white medium weight paper and glue the chimney on it.

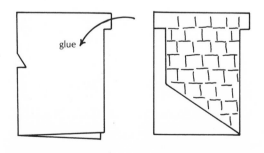

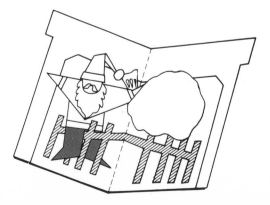

13   Glue the white paper on the front of the card.

ORIGAMI GIFT WRAPPINGS

Reindeer

MATERIALS			
	TYPE OF PAPER	NUMBER OF SHEETS	DIMENSIONS OF EACH SHEET
REINDEER A (HEAD)	Yellow-green, light weight	1	3″ × 3″
REINDEER BODY	Yellow-green, light weight	1	3″ × 3″

Other materials: 25″ of gold ribbon; 6″ × 4″ × ¾″ box· glue.

Make a reindeer A (see p. 82) with yellow-green paper. Draw the eyes.

(see p. 82)

1

back side

Make the reindeer's body and write your holiday greeting on it.

2

Glue the reindeer's face and body on the box and tie with ribbon.

Chrysanthemum

MATERIALS			
	TYPE OF PAPER	NUMBER OF SHEETS	DIMENSIONS OF EACH SHEET
CHRYSAN-THEMUM	Gold and silver striped foil	1	7½″ × 7½″
	Gold and black striped foil	1	7½″ × 7½″
	Gold foil	1	⅜″ diameter
BOX	Purple dotted, medium weight	2	16⅞″ × 6″

Other materials: 6½″ of gold cord; glue.

Glue gold and silver striped paper and gold and black striped paper back-to-back. Make a chrysanthemum (see p. 42). Glue the circular piece of gold foil onto the center of the chrysanthemum.

(see p. 42)

1

6″

16⅞″   3⅜″

Cut two parallelograms out of purple paper, as shown.

2

Fold each parallelogram into a triangle.

3

Place the triangles on top of each other as shown. Attach gold cord as shown.

7″

Tie cord

4

Glue the chrysanthemum to the center.

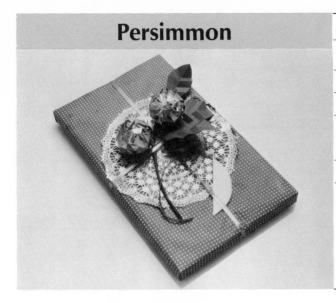

Persimmon

MATERIALS

	TYPE OF PAPER	NUMBER OF SHEETS	DIMENSIONS OF EACH SHEET
PERSIMMONS	Gold striped foil	2	6¾″ × 6¾″
CALYCES	Green, medium weight	2	¾″ × ¾″
LEAVES	Green, medium weight	2	3″ × 2¼″
	Green, medium weight	1	2½″ × 1½″
GIFT TAG	White, medium weight	1	4″ × 2¼″

Other materials: 2 1¼″ long green floral wires;
2 3½″ long green floral wires;
1 3¼″ long green floral wires;
3 12″ long green floral wires; green adhesive tape;
1 gold lace paper doily (8″ diameter);
50″ of gold ribbon; glue.

Make two persimmons (see p. 52) with gold striped foil.

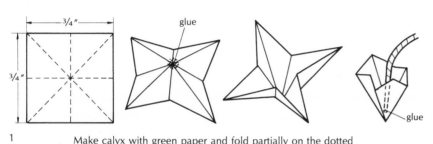

1
Make calyx with green paper and fold partially on the dotted lines as shown. Glue 1¼″ wire to the center of calyx. Repeat for second calyx.

2
Glue calyces to persimmons.

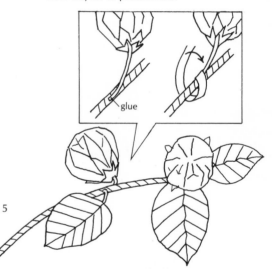

3
Make one small and two large leaves with green paper, cutting off the shaded parts. Score the dotted lines with blunt scissors. Fold in "accordion" creases as shown, and then unfold completely.

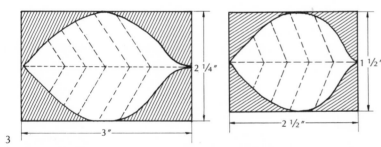

4
Glue two 3½″ wires onto the two large leaves. Glue the 3¼″ wire onto the small leaf.

5
Wrap three 12″ wires together with green tape. Glue the stems of persimmons and leaves to this thick 12″ wire to make a branch, and wrap the wire with green tape again.

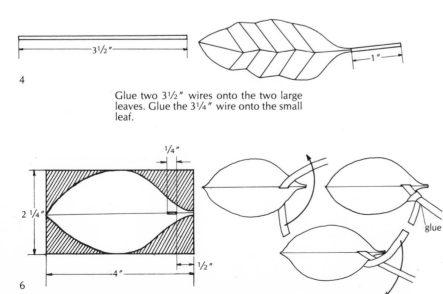

6
Cut out a gift tag and attach ribbon to it.

7
Put gold lace paper doily on a box, tie ribbon, and insert persimmon branch. Attach gift tag.

Poinsettia

MATERIALS

	TYPE OF PAPER	NUMBER OF SHEETS	DIMENSIONS OF EACH SHEET
POINSETTIAS	Gold striped foil	5	6″ × 6″
GIFT TAG	White, medium weight	1	2½″ × 2½″

Other materials: 1 white lace paper doily (7″ diameter); 40″ of yellow ribbon; 6″ – 8″ of gold ribbon; 4″ × 4″ × 4″ box; glue.

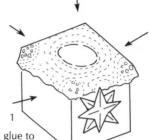

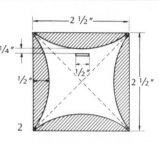

Make five poinsettias (see p. 58) with gold foil.

Put a white lace paper doily on the top of box. Apply glue to the front of each poinsettia, and affix one poinsettia to each side and the top of the box. The back sides of the poinsettias should face out.

Cut out a gift tag. Fold on the dotted lines, then unfold it and gather it at the center to make a starshape.

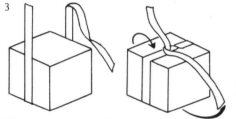

Tie ribbon and attach gift tag (see p. 143).

Camellia

MATERIALS

		TYPE OF PAPER	NUMBER OF SHEETS	DIMENSIONS OF EACH SHEET
LID		Cardboard	1	6½″ × 6½″
		Silver striped, light weight	1	12″ × 12″
		Black and gold striped, light weight	1	12″ × 12″
		Red, light weight	1	3″ × 3″
GIFT TAG		Gray or silver, light weight	1	3¾″ × 3¾″
BOTTOM OF BOX		Cardboard	1	6½″ × 6½″
		Black and gold striped, light weight	1	6″ × 6″
		Silver striped, light weight	1	6½″ × 6½″
SIDES AND INSIDE OF BOX		Cardboard	8	2⁷⁄₁₆″ × 2¾″
		Silver striped, light weight	1	21½″ × 3¹³⁄₁₆″
		Black and gold striped, light weight	1	19½″ × 2¾″

Other materials: 10″–11″ of silver cord; adhesive tape; glue.

Lid of box:

1a. Cut an octagon out of 6½″ × 6½″ cardboard, making the sides 2⅝″ each.

1b. Glue 12″ × 12″ silver striped paper and black and gold striped paper back-to-back. Make a camellia (see p. 55). When you begin to fold, be sure that the black and gold striped paper faces you; the front of the finished camellia will be of silver striped paper.

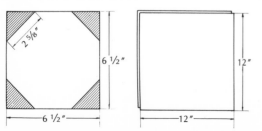

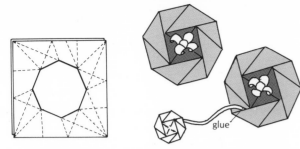

1c. Completely unfold the camellia and you'll see a small octagon in the center. Place the octagon from step 1a in the center and refold camellia. Make a rose (see p. 44) with red paper and glue it onto the center of camellia.

1d. For the gift tag, make a small camellia (see p. 55) with gray or silver paper. Glue one end of silver cord on the back, and glue other end of cord inside a petal of the camellia on lid.

Bottom of box:

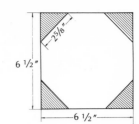

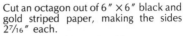

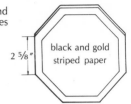

2a

Cut an octagon out of 6″ × 6″ black and gold striped paper, making the sides 2⁷/₁₆″ each.

2b

Cut an octagon out of 6½″ × 6½″ cardboard, making the sides 2⁵/₈″ each.

black and gold striped paper

2c

Glue the octagon from step 2a on the cardboard octagon from step 2b. This will be the inside bottom of box.

Sides and inside of box:

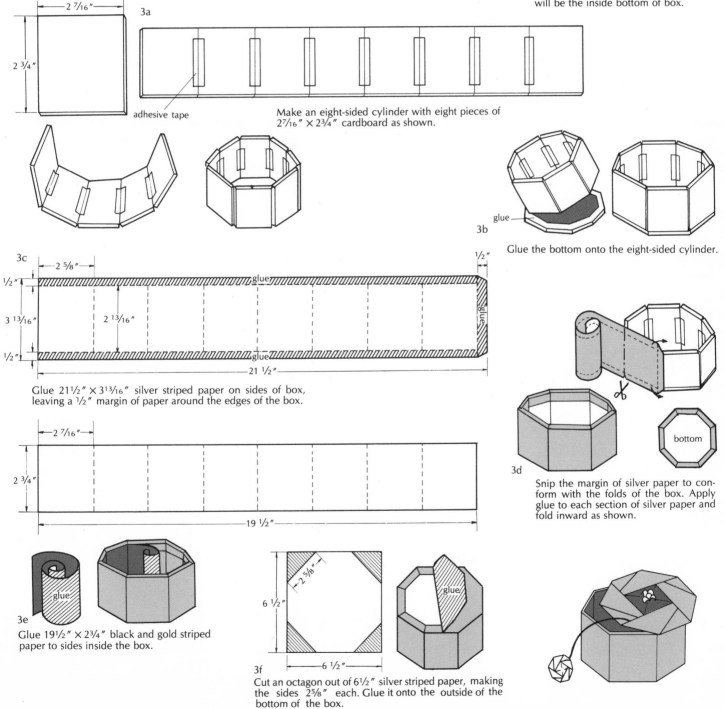

3a

adhesive tape

Make an eight-sided cylinder with eight pieces of 2⁷/₁₆″ × 2³/₄″ cardboard as shown.

3b

Glue the bottom onto the eight-sided cylinder.

3c

Glue 21½″ × 3¹³/₁₆″ silver striped paper on sides of box, leaving a ½″ margin of paper around the edges of the box.

3d

Snip the margin of silver paper to conform with the folds of the box. Apply glue to each section of silver paper and fold inward as shown.

3e

Glue 19½″ × 2³/₄″ black and gold striped paper to sides inside the box.

3f

Cut an octagon out of 6½″ silver striped paper, making the sides 2⁵/₈″ each. Glue it onto the outside of the bottom of the box.

FLOWER BALL ORNAMENTS

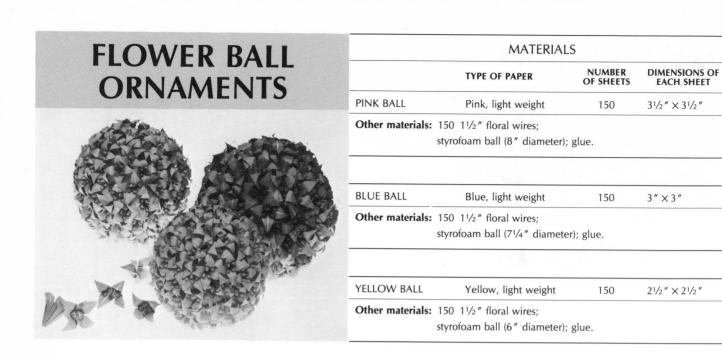

MATERIALS			
	TYPE OF PAPER	NUMBER OF SHEETS	DIMENSIONS OF EACH SHEET
PINK BALL	Pink, light weight	150	3½″ × 3½″
Other materials: 150 1½″ floral wires; styrofoam ball (8″ diameter); glue.			
BLUE BALL	Blue, light weight	150	3″ × 3″
Other materials: 150 1½″ floral wires; styrofoam ball (7¼″ diameter); glue.			
YELLOW BALL	Yellow, light weight	150	2½″ × 2½″
Other materials: 150 1½″ floral wires; styrofoam ball (6″ diameter); glue.			

Make irises (see p. 48) with pink, blue, and yellow paper.

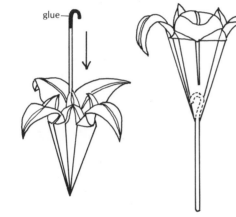

1

Bend wire, apply glue to end, and insert wire into iris as shown.

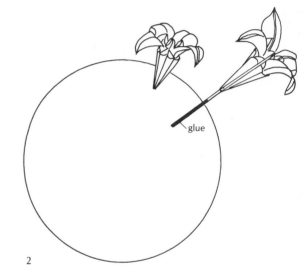

2

Apply glue to other end of wire, and stick wire into styrofoam ball.

3

Continue to glue irises to wires and stick them into the styrofoam ball base until it is completely covered.

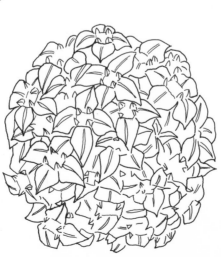

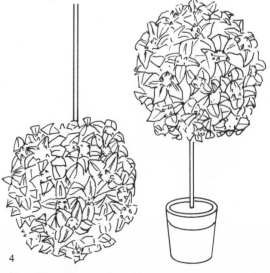

4

Use a bent wire or a thread loop to hang ornament, or insert a stick into the ball and stand it in a flower-pot filled with sand or soil.

FESTIVE BOUQUET

MATERIALS

	TYPE OF PAPER	NUMBER OF SHEETS	DIMENSIONS OF EACH SHEET
CARNATIONS	Red, gray, blue yellow, pink, and purple, light weight	60	6″ × 6″ 5″ × 5″ 4″ × 4″
ROSES	Red, gray, blue, yellow, pink, and purple, light weight	40	6″ × 6″ 5″ × 5″ 4″ × 4″
IRISES	Red, gray, blue, yellow, pink, and purple, light weight	60	6″ × 6″ 5″ × 5″ 4″ × 4″

Other materials: 160 appropriately colored floral wires, each 12″–14″ long; glue.

Make carnations (see p. 38), roses (see p. 44), and irises (see p. 48), varying the colors and the sizes for each type of flower. In the photograph there are about 160 blossoms.

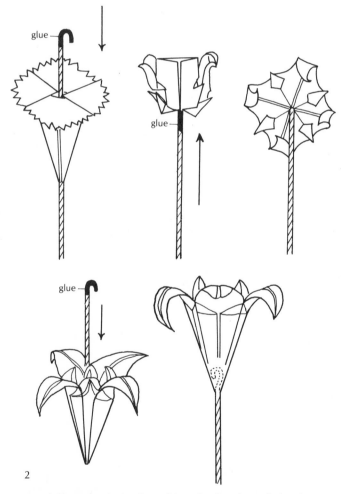

Attach flowers and wires by making a hook at the end of each wire, applying glue, and inserting it in the flower as shown. (Flowers and wires should be the same color.)

1

Make stems for flowers with appropriately colored floral wire, or by wrapping colored tape around #20 flexible wire in an even spiral.

3

Place the flowers in a flower vase.